The Iroquois

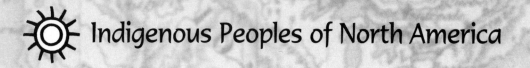
The Iroquois

Lydia Bjornlund

Lucent Books, Inc.
P.O. Box 289011, San Diego, California

Titles in the Indigenous Peoples of North America Series Include:

The Apache
The Cherokee
The Cheyenne
The Comanche
The Iroquois
Native Americans of the Great Lakes
Native Americans of the Northeast
Native Americans of the Northwest Coast
Native Americans of the Plains
Native Americans of the Southeast
Native Americans of the Southwest
The Navajo
The Sioux

Library of Congress Cataloging-in-Publication Data

Bjornlund, Lydia.
    The Iroquois / by Lydia Bjornlund.
        p.   cm. — (Indigenous peoples of North America)
    Includes bibliographical references and index.
    Summary: Discusses the origins, way of life, spirituality, and social organization of the Iroquois nations, as well as their relationships with the European settlers.
    ISBN 1-56006-618-0 (hardcover : alk. paper)
    1. Iroquois Indians—History—Juvenile literature.   2. Iroquois Indians—Social life and customs—Juvenile literature [1. Iroquois Indians. 2. Indians of North America—New York (State)]
I. Title. II. Series.
  E99.I7 B57 2001
  974.7004'9755—dc21   99-050908

Copyright 2001 by Lucent Books, Inc.
P.O. Box 289011, San Diego, California 92198-9011

Printed in the U.S.A.

Contents

Foreword

North America's native peoples are often relegated to history—viewed primarily as remnants of another era—or cast in the stereotypical images long found in popular entertainment and even literature. Efforts to characterize Native Americans typically result in idealized portrayals of spiritualists communing with nature or bigoted descriptions of savages incapable of living in civilized society. Lost in these unfortunate images is the rich variety of customs, beliefs, and values that comprised—and still comprise—many of North America's native populations.

The *Indigenous Peoples of North America* series strives to present a complex, realistic picture of the many and varied Native American cultures. Each book in the series offers historical perspectives as well as a view of contemporary life of individual tribes and tribes that share a common region. The series examines traditional family life, spirituality, interaction with other native and non-native peoples, warfare, and the ways the environment shaped the lives and cultures of North America's indigenous populations. Each book ends with a discussion of life today for the Native Americans of a given region or tribe.

In any discussion of the Native American experience, there are bound to be sim-

ilarities. All tribes share a past filled with unceasing white expansion and resistance that led to more than four hundred years of conflict. One U.S. administration after another pursued this goal and fought Indians who attempted to defend their homelands and ways of life. Although no war was ever formally declared, the U.S. policy of conquest precluded any chance of white and Native American peoples living together peacefully. Between 1780 and 1890, Americans killed hundreds of thousands of Indians and wiped out whole tribes.

The Indians lost the fight for their land and ways of life, though not for lack of bravery, skill, or a sense of purpose. They simply could not contend with the overwhelming numbers of whites arriving from Europe or the superior weapons they brought with them. Lack of unity also contributed to the defeat of the Native Americans. For most, tribal identity was more important than racial identity. This loyalty left the Indians at a distinct disadvantage. Whites had a strong racial identity and they fought alongside each other even when there was disagreement because they shared a racial destiny.

Although all Native Americans share this tragic history they have many distinct differences. For example, some tribes and individuals sought to cooperate almost immediately with the U.S. government while others steadfastly resisted the white presence. Life before the arrival of white settlers also varied. The nomads of the Plains developed altogether different lifestyles and customs from the fishermen of the Northwest coast.

Contemporary life is no different in this regard. Many Native Americans—forced onto reservations by the American government—struggle with poverty, poor health, and inferior schooling. But others have regained a sense of pride in themselves and their heritage, enabling them to search out new routes to self-sufficiency and prosperity.

The *Indigenous Peoples of North America* series attempts to capture the differences as well as similarities that make up the experiences of North America's native populations—both past and present. Fully documented primary and secondary source quotations enliven the text. Sidebars highlight events, personalities, and traditions. Bibliographies provide readers with ideas for further research. In all, each book in this dynamic series provides students with a wealth of information as well as launching points for further research.

Who Are the Iroquois?

Anthropologists believe the Iroquois are descendants of Asian peoples who crossed the land bridge over the Bering Strait during the Ice Age. Gradually, bands of these people migrated eastward, and the ancestors of the Iroquois traveled nearly across the continent, settling in the area that is now upstate New York perhaps as long ago as A.D. 1100. Centuries before the first white settlers reached the shores of the New World, the Iroquois had established villages in the region between the Adirondack Mountains and Niagara Falls.

Although the majority of their villages remained in upstate New York, by the late seventeenth century the Iroquois had gained control of lands as far west as Kentucky, the junction of the Ohio and Mississippi Rivers, and the southern tip of Lake Michigan; as far north as southern Ontario and Quebec; as far east as the Connecticut River; and as far south as Pennsylvania and the Chesapeake Bay.

From One People to Many

Based on the study of Iroquoian languages, experts conclude that most of the Native American groups in the northeastern region of the United States and the southern portions of Ontario and Quebec came from the same ancestors. As these peoples moved outward and established individual villages, they grew apart, forming separate identities and loyalties. This was a slow process that took place over many generations. Similarities in the languages of the Oneida and the Mohawk, for example, suggest that they may have been one group as late as the fifteenth century.

So, who are the Iroquois? The term generally refers to the nations that joined together in an alliance of mutual support to protect themselves against their enemies. Historians know that this alliance—the so-called Iroquois confederacy—was in place by the mid–sixteenth century, and some have estimated that it was formed a century or more earlier. The five member nations were the Cayuga, Mohawk, Oneida, Onondaga, and Seneca. In 1722 the Tuscarora, who had migrated north from South Carolina after war with English colonists, were added as a sixth, nonvoting member. Before the Tuscarora joined, the confederacy was often called the League of Five Nations (or simply, the Five Nations). After 1722, it became known as the League of Six Nations (or the Six Nations).

A number of other groups shared the Iroquoian language and culture. These include the five nations of the Huron confederacy, the five nations of the Neutral confederacy, some of the Erie, and the Petun, Wenro, and Susquehannock.

Before they were uprooted by European settlers in the seventeenth and eighteenth centuries, all of these Iroquoian-speaking tribes together numbered ninety thousand to one hundred thousand people. About one-fifth of this total were members of the Five Nations.

The Influence of the Iroquois

The Iroquois' influence on early colonial history in America belies their relatively small numbers. The confederacy gave them strength and power that most neighboring tribes lacked. They became spokesmen for other northeastern tribes, often playing one European power off of

The Mohawk is one of the nations that joined the Iroquois confederacy for protection against its enemies. In the Mohawk village shown here, tepees and wooden structures have replaced the traditional longhouse.

another to strike the best bargain. "The Iroquois are some of the most famous Indians in American history and justly so," writes anthropologist Ruth M. Underhill:

> Their government was the most integrated and orderly north of Mexico, and some have even thought it gave suggestions to the American Constitution (Lee, Franklin, Jefferson, and Washington were quite familiar with the League). They developed what came close to an empire, with conquered nations paying tribute and taking their orders. For over a hundred years they held a pivotal position in America between the French and the English. It seems very possible that, except for the Iroquois, North America at this day might have been French.[1]

While it may be difficult to speculate what might have occurred if the Iroquois had not been present when the French, English, and American settlers fought over their territory, there is no doubt that this powerful people left a lasting legacy.

Chapter 1

The Iroquois: Past and Present

Today, more than seventy thousand members of the six Iroquois nations live in the United States and Canada, primarily near the border between the two countries. These are descendants of an agricultural people who called themselves Hodenosaunee (ho-dee-noe-sho-nee), or "People of the Longhouse," a name derived from the long, bark-covered communal dwellings in which they lived. The name that now identifies them, however, came from their enemies. Local Algonquians and other peoples used the word "Hilokoa," meaning "Killer People," a blunt reference

An Iroquois man stands in the doorway of a traditional longhouse.

to the fierce nature of the Iroquois tribes. French explorers and traders adopted Hilokoa, which they spelled Iroquois, to fit their own pronunciation (ee-ro-kwa).

The term Iroquois generally refers to the six nations of the Iroquois confederacy, a loosely knit alliance of tribes that speak a related language and share a similar culture. The confederacy is sometimes likened to a longhouse, with the Mohawk at the east and the Seneca at the west. The other nations making up the Iroquois confederacy are the Oneida, the Onondaga, and the Cayuga. The Tuscarora joined as a sixth nation in the early eighteenth century.

Like other Native Americans who lived in what is now the eastern United States, the Iroquois' way of life was profoundly affected by European exploration and settlement. Although their population had reached a peak in the mid–seventeenth century, their numbers were soon decimated by the guns and disease brought by white men and by the intensified warfare that resulted. The confederacy that allowed the Iroquois to thrive amid their Native American enemies was not strong enough to withstand the tumult of the American Revolution and the new settlers' thirst for land. Some Iroquois abandoned their villages to move west or north; others stayed to forge treaties with their new neighbors. Most ended up ceding their land to the United States or selling their land to speculators for a pittance, moving to small reservations in New York and Ontario, where they continue to live today.

What's in a Name?

Like Iroquois, the Mohawk tribe was given its name by its enemies; the Narragansett Indians called them Mohowaanuck, which means "Man Eaters." The Mohawk called themselves Kanyenkehaka, which is usually translated as "People of the Flint" but may also mean "Place of the Crystals," referring to their role as suppliers of quartz crystals, which the Iroquois believed symbolized health and success. The Mohawk were also spoken of within the League of Five Nations as the "Keepers of the Eastern Door" in reference to their location to the east of other tribes.

Harmen van den Bogaert, an early Dutch traveler, referred to all Iroquois west of the Mohawk as Sinnekin, but the name Seneca later came to identify just the people who called themselves the Onontowaka, which means "People of the Big Hill" or "Great Hill People." Because they occupied the westernmost land of the five Iroquois nations, the Seneca also were sometimes called the "Keepers of the Western Door."

The names of the other Iroquois tribes are European derivations of their own names for themselves, which describe the locations of their villages. Oneida, for example, comes from Oneyoteaka, or "People of the Standing Stone." Oneyoteaka was also what they called their single village, which was located near a large boulder. Onondaga is a derivation of Onontakeka, which means "People of the Hill." The meaning of Kayohkhono, which became Cayuga, is not known, but some historians have suggested that it meant "People at the Landing" or "People of the

☀ Iroquoian Speakers: Beyond the Five Iroquois Nations

The Iroquois Confederacy consisted of five, and then six, Iroquoian-speaking tribes, but there were several other Native American groups that spoke a similar language. The Huron, for example, who lived west of the Iroquois in the Upper Great Lakes region, spoke an Iroquoian dialect, leading linguists to believe that they and the Iroquois nations evolved from common ancestors. Like the Iroquois, the Huron joined several tribes in a confederacy, but they never became as strong. Their name was given to them by French fur traders and derives from a French word meaning "wild boar," but more often signifying "savage." They called themselves Wendat, or "People Who Live on a Peninsula," after the land on which they lived.

Other Iroquoian-speaking nations included the Erie, who occupied the southeastern edge of the lake named for them; the Susquehannock, or "People at the Falls," who inhabited the Susquehanna River valley in New York until they migrated to Pennsylvania in the mid–sixteenth century; and the Petun, or "Tobacco Peo-

ple," who lived west of the Hurons below Georgian Bay. The Neutral confederacy, a coalition of groups (probably five), occupied land from the western shores of Lake Ontario eastward to the Niagara River. They earned their name because they avoided the constant warfare between the Iroquois and the Huron.

There were several Iroquoian groups that existed at the time of the first European contact but disappeared shortly thereafter. When Jacques Cartier first explored the St. Lawrence in 1535, he reported finding at least eleven villages of Iroquoian-speaking Indians between present-day Quebec and Montreal. Montreal, then called Hochelaga, was perhaps the largest; more than three thousand people lived within its fortified walls. When the French returned to the area in 1603, however, Hochelaga and the other villages had disappeared. The villagers were likely absorbed into larger, stronger groups. Some historians believe that these St. Lawrence Iroquois were related to the Huron and incorporated into the Huron confederacy.

Mucky Land," a description of the land between the Cayuga and Owasco Lakes where the Cayuga villages are located. In league affairs they were often referred to as the "People of the Great Pipe."

The sixth nation to become part of the Iroquois league, the Tuscarora, were an Iroquoian-speaking tribe that had settled in North Carolina. As European settlers began to encroach on their lands in the early eighteenth century, the Tuscarora fled to join their Iroquois relatives in western New York. In 1722, they were recognized as part of the Iroquois confederacy. Tuscarora, which means "Shirt-Wearing People," may have highlighted differences in dress from other people in the region.

Iroquois Villages

The Iroquois tribes lived in fortified hilltop villages. Unlike Plains Indians, who frequently camped and decamped to follow buffalo herds, Iroquois villages were semipermanent. French explorer Samuel de Champlain, who was one of the first Europeans to come into contact with the Iroquois, wrote in 1615, "They sometimes change their villages at intervals of ten, twenty, or thirty years, and transfer them to a distance of one, two, or three leagues for the preceding situation, except when compelled by their enemies to dislodge, in which case they retire to a greater distance."[2] The Iroquois moved their villages only when the soil was no longer fertile, when hunting grounds were exhausted, or when they decided that their village could not be adequately defended from attack.

And attacks were to be expected, for the Iroquois were a fierce, warlike people. Indeed, proving himself as a warrior was one of the primary ways for a man to earn respect and gain prestige. The Iroquois confederacy brought peace among five Iroquoian-speaking nations, but these nations continued to fight bitterly with their non-Iroquois neighbors. They also conducted raids to bring home captives to replace the loss of loved ones. Iroquois hunting grounds extended well beyond the confines of

their villages, so competition over hunting grounds was a main source of conflict. Later, the rivalry would extend to trade with the French and other Europeans.

As fighting among the Indians of the region intensified, smaller villages merged to form more powerful units. The Onondaga are the first of the Iroquois tribes that can be positively identified in New York, dating from the merger of two small villages between 1450 and 1475. The Onondaga gradually concentrated into two major communities. The Seneca also settled in two primary villages, which relocated periodically. By 1634, the Mohawk had established four large villages.

French explorer Samuel de Champlain.

The Seneca Nation of Indians

The Seneca split into two factions when some abandoned the traditional system of governance for a system by which leaders were elected. Today, the traditional system of government is practiced at Tonawanda and Buffalo Creek, while the Allegany and Cattaraugus Reservations use an elected system. Other Iroquois tribes also have split on which form of government is best suited for their needs. The following excerpt from the Seneca Nation of Indians' (SNI) webpage offers insight into their system of government and economic structure today.

"The Seneca Nation of Indians came into formal existence in 1848 when they abolished the 'chief' system and established a constitution with elected officials. The constitution provides for an Executive Branch, a Legislative Branch, and a Judicial Branch. The Executive Branch is comprised of the President, Treasurer and Clerk, who are elected every two years and may not succeed themselves. The Legislative Branch (or Tribal Council) is comprised of 16 members; eight from the Cattaraugus Reservation and eight from the Allegany Reservation, who are elected for four-year staggered terms. The Judiciary Branch is comprised of separate Peacemaker, Appellate, and Surrogate Courts.

The Seneca Nation government is a true democracy. In fact, most of the United States government is based on the democratic style of the Iroquois Nations. . . . Under the leadership of elected officials, the Seneca Nation of Indians has generated revenue through a variety of means, including a number of leases entered into by the tribe and various enterprises. . . . The Seneca Nation of Indians . . . employs people in several Tribal departments, including jobs that range from maintenance and custodial to management and executive positions, as well as a number of positions for the various SNI enterprises. . . . SNI enterprises include "Seneca One Stop" convenience stores on each of the SNI Reservations, Seneca Bingo Halls, and Highbanks Campgrounds located on the [Allegany Indian Reservation]. Each of these businesses employs its own staff of mostly enrolled Senecas. Also located on the [Cattaraugus Indian Reservation] is an indoor sports arena available for recreation, practice and/or competition. There are also a variety of privately owned enterprises, ranging from gas stations and smoke shops to diners and convenience stores.

Other forms of economic independence result from monies received through various land leases that the SNI has entered into on behalf of its members. Along with this revenue, monies are also being received from the federal and state governments through a settlement pertaining to past inequities of the lease between the City of Salamanca and the SNI. The settlement was passed by the U.S. Congress (Public Law 101-503), and provides for certain amounts of money to be allocated for future economic development."

By the time of European contact, many Iroquois villages were home to as many as two thousand people and encompassed several acres. The Iroquois built most of their villages on high ground so that they could better see enemy tribes approaching. (Later, they would move closer to waterways to have better access to the fur trade.) To further protect themselves from attack, they fortified the villages with rows of wooden palisades reaching high into the air. Beyond the palisades, the villagers sometimes dug ditches as additional protection. The Dutch and English settlers who first came upon these villages referred to them as castles.

Population Trends

The Iroquois population reached its peak during the seventeenth century. In 1600, an estimated twenty thousand people composed the five Iroquois nations. The Mohawk, who numbered about seventy-seven hundred at the height of their population, were the most numerous of the five.

Contact with Europeans spelled disaster for the Iroquois, however. Like other Native American groups, they suffered from the diseases that the Europeans brought—new diseases against which their bodies did not have time to build resistance. In addition, as they began to compete with their neighbors for trading rights with Europeans and acquired European firearms, the intertribal warfare became increasingly deadly. By 1650, their population had been cut in half.

The Iroquois population increased somewhat during the second half of the seventeenth century, largely due to the adoption of massive numbers of Iroquoian speakers. In one instance, a band of more than five hundred Huron refugees was incorporated into the Seneca nation, where they started a village of their own. "I am going to my country, to seek out my relatives and

Huron refugees helped increase the Iroquois population during the late seventeenth century. Present-day members of the Huron tribe are shown here in traditional dress.

friends," explained a Huron captive, pleading for refuge with a Mohawk war party. "The country of the Huron is no longer where it was—you have transported it into your own."[3] As a result of this mass adoption, the Five Nations reached its height in 1660, numbering approximately twenty-five thousand people.

The Iroquois were less inclined to adopt members of non-Iroquian-speaking tribes, however, and began to witness further decline in population after 1660. Even after the Iroquois confederacy expanded in 1722 to include fifteen hundred to two thousand Tuscarora, the Iroquois population continued to decrease. There were only about twelve thousand Iroquois in 1768, and less than half that number at the end of the century.

Mohawk leader Joseph Brant led many Iroquois into Canada during the late eighteenth century.

Location and Relocation

Colonists began in earnest to encroach on the Iroquois' New York lands in the mid–eighteenth century. As Europeans and then Americans spread westward, the Indians struggled to keep their lands and maintain their way of life. They made treaty after treaty with the white man and worked with other Native American tribes to come to agreements by which all could live.

The American Revolution had a devastating effect on the Iroquois. Both the English and the Americans attempted to win over the Six Nations. Some groups sided with the British forces, while others joined the Americans, resulting in a behind-the-scenes Iroquoian civil war. The Revolutionary War also ravaged the land on which the Iroquois lived; only two villages remained unaffected by the fighting.

Postwar treaties stripped the Iroquois of their sovereignty and deprived them of their land. Mohawk leader Joseph Brant led a massive exodus of Iroquois from New York to Canada, where small settlements of Mohawk had been formed before and during the Revolutionary War. In addition to most of the surviving Mohawk, the exodus included a significant number of Cayuga and others from the Six Nations. Roughly half of the Iroquois population—including most of the Mohawk—have since resided in Canada.

Under increasing pressure by state officials and land speculators who saw fortunes to be made in opening up the land for settlement, many Iroquois chiefs sold their land for far less than its worth. In 1785 the Oneida and Tuscarora sold 1,600 square miles for $15,500. The Seneca at first resisted turning over their land, but in the end ceded all but about 310 square miles to the Holland Land Company. The Onondaga sold off much of their land as well, but kept 6,100 acres in central New York State, which continues to serve as their reservation today.

The Cayuga and Oneida also were unsuccessful in holding on to their land. The Cayuga sold their land in 1807 and moved west to Ohio, where they settled with the Mingo—Iroquoian speakers who had earlier separated from the Iroquois. In 1831 this combined group left Ohio and relocated to Indian Territory, or present-day Oklahoma. The Oneida yielded to pressure to relocate in 1838; most of them moved to a reservation near Green Bay, Wisconsin, where they continue to live today.

Where Are They Now?

With more than 35,000 members, today the Mohawk are the largest group of Iroquois. About 7,700 Mohawk live on a reservation that straddles the New York–Quebec border—more than two-thirds live on the Canadian side. In addition, almost 12,000 Mohawk live in Ontario, many on the Grand River Reserve (reserve is the Canadian term for reservation), a plot of land near Brantford that was set aside for the Iroquois in the 1880s. Significant numbers of Mohawk live in Quebec. In addition, there is a large population of Mohawk in Brooklyn, New York, where they have traditionally dominated the trade as structural ironworkers.

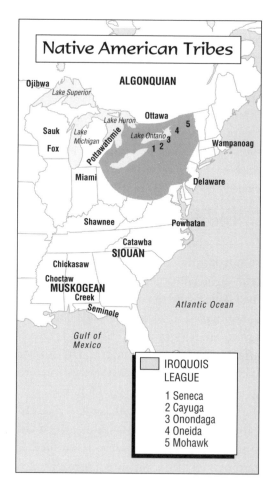

Native American Tribes

Ojibwa
Lake Superior
ALGONQUIAN
Ottawa
Lake Huron
Sauk
Lake Michigan
Lake Ontario
Pottawatomie
1 2 3 4 5
Wampanoag
Fox
Miami
Delaware
Shawnee
Powhatan
Catawba
SIOUAN
Chickasaw
Choctaw
MUSKOGEAN
Creek
Seminole
Atlantic Ocean
Gulf of Mexico

IROQUOIS LEAGUE

1 Seneca
2 Cayuga
3 Onondaga
4 Oneida
5 Mohawk

The Seneca were at one time the largest tribe of the League of Five Nations; today they number about 9,100. More than a thousand live on the Grand River Reserve. The Seneca also reside on several smaller Seneca reservations in western New York: The Seneca nation operates the Cattaraugus Reservation, which encompasses about 21,618 acres in Cattaraugus, Chautauqua, and Erie Counties, and the Allegany Reservation, 20,469 acres along the Allegheny River. It is on the Allegany Reservation that Salamanca—the only American city owned by a Native American nation—can be found. Seneca also reside on the Buffalo Creek and the Tonawanda Reservations. The Seneca at these two reservations are not part of the Seneca nation; rather they maintain their political affiliation with the New York League of Iroquois.

Once one of the smallest Iroquois tribes, the Oneida currently number about 16,000. In addition to the 11,000 living in Wisconsin, about 4,600 live in Ontario, another 700 live on a small reservation in New York, and most of the rest live with the Onondaga.

There are just 3,000 Cayuga in Canada and 500 in the United States. Most of the Cayuga in Canada are on the Six Nations Reserve; most in the United States live with the Seneca on New York reservations. Some of the descendents of those who went to live

The Mohawk (shown here) are the largest group of Iroquois and live along the New York–Quebec border.

with the Mingo also live among the Seneca-Cayuga tribe in northeastern Oklahoma.

The populations of the Onondaga and the Tuscarora are even smaller. About 1,600 Onondaga live today in New York, mostly in or near a small reservation just south of Syracuse. About 1,200 Tuscarora live on

Iroquois Population Decline

The seventeenth and eighteenth centuries witnessed a decline in the populations of all five Iroquois nations, but the Iroquois often bolstered their numbers with numbers of captives from other tribes. The following population estimates are from Dean R. Snow's book, *The Iroquois*.

Year	Seneca	Cayuga	Onondaga	Oneida	Mohawk	Total
1630	4,000	4,000	4,000	2,000	7,740	21,740
1640	4,000	2,000	2,000	1,000	2,835	11,835
1650	4,000	1,200	1,200	600	1,734	8,734
1660	4,000	1,200	1,200	400	2,304	9,184
1670	4,000	1,200	1,300	600	1,985	9,085
1680	4,000	1,200	1,400	800	1,000	8,400
1690	4,000	1,200	2,000	720	1,000	8,920
1700	2,400	800	1,000	280	620	5,100
1710	4,000	600	1,400	480	620	7,100
1720	2,800	520	1,000	800	580	5,700
1730	1,400	480	800	400	580	3,660
1740	2,000	500	800	400	580	4,280
1750	2,000	500	800	800	580	4,680
1760	4,200	504	544	1,000	640	6,888
1770	4,000	1,040	800	800	640	7,280

the Tuscarora Reservation near Niagara Falls. Another 600 Onondaga and 200 Tuscarora live on reservations in Canada.

Like other Native Americans, many Iroquois have moved to cities where they live and work alongside the many races and cultures alive in present-day America. In addition to the Mohawk in Brooklyn, the largest nonreservation Iroquois populations in New York State are in Buffalo, Niagara Falls, and Rochester. Large numbers of Iroquois are also in the Canadian cities of Montreal and Quebec.

From the Past to the Future

Despite the fact that they have lived among whites for more than four hundred years, the Iroquois have managed to keep intact much of their culture and traditions. In part, their strength comes from a profound sense of sovereignty and pride in their rich history. John Long, an Englishman, wrote of the Iroquois after meeting them in the seventeenth century:

The Iroquois laugh when you talk to them of obedience to kings; for they cannot reconcile the idea of submission with the dignity of man. Each individual is a sovereign in his own mind; and as he conceives he derives his freedom from the [Creator] alone, he cannot be induced to acknowledge any other power.[4]

Another author writes that the Iroquois "share a conviction that theirs was the first union of American states, and that spirit persists whenever Iroquois come together to honor their traditions of peace and power."[5]

Like other American Indians, however, the Iroquois have not been able to continue their traditional way of life. Stripped of their agricultural lands and hunting grounds, they have had to forge new lives, whether on their reservations or in urban communities. In the matter of a few decades, the coming of the white man destroyed the complex society that had evolved over centuries and enabled the Iroquois to flourish.

Chapter 2

People of the Longhouse

Prior to European colonization, the Iroquois exercised active dominion over most of what is now New York State. This was a land of plenty—what one historian calls "some of the most beautiful and resource wealthy lands in all of North America."[6] It was covered with forests, and the Indians who lived there learned to capitalize on the bounty the forests provided. The Iroquois used the nearby timber, bark, and wood to build their homes and canoes; to carve bows and arrow shafts to fell their prey; and to craft baskets to gather their food, bark-lined containers in which to store it, wooden bowls from which to eat, and many other household items. The Iroquois' respect for the environment in which they lived can be seen in the symbols that the Iroquois adopted. The pine tree, for example, became the symbol of the lasting strength of the Iroquois confederacy.

The abundance of animal and plant life in the lush forests also provided the Iroquois with the dietary sustenance they needed to thrive. Over time, however, the Iroquois evolved from a hunting and gathering society to well-developed agricultural communities. As a result, by the sixteenth century the Iroquois way of life was stable and efficient. Labor was divided among women and men: The women tilled the soil, prepared the food, and tended to the children, while the men hunted and fished, raided other villages, and made treaties with other nations.

The Longhouse

The life of the Iroquois revolved around the longhouse in which they lived. Iroquois longhouses could be as large as two hundred feet long and twenty feet wide. They were built using a framework of poles covered with bark that had been peeled from elm trees in the spring and stacked in strips to flatten. One early European explorer described the making of the longhouse:

As to their huts, they are built like arbors. They drive into the ground very long poles as thick as one's leg and join them to one another by making them curve and bend over at the top; they tie and fasten them together with basswood bark. . . . They then entwine with these large poles crosspieces as thick as one's arm and cover them from top to bottom with the bark of firs and cedars.[7]

Each longhouse was the home of as many as twenty extended families—members of the same clan linked through their mothers to a common ancestor. Inside the longhouse, a wide central hallway ran from one end to the other. On each end of the longhouse was a wide door, covered with bark to keep out the cold. Smokeholes,

which were placed every twenty feet or so for the length of the building, provided the only other ventilation. Under each smokehole, families carved out a hearth for fires, which were used for cooking and for heat. Each hearth was shared by the two nuclear families (consisting of a mother, father, and children) who lived on either side of the hallway. Often, a storage area was added at the end of the longhouse. Storage areas were usually built as temporary structures so that they could be easily torn down if there was a need to accommodate additional families in the longhouse.

As many as twenty extended families shared hearths inside the Iroquois longhouse.

23

The Longhouse

Early European visitors to Iroquois villages described the longhouse in some detail. The descriptions often complain of the cramped nature of the quarters, as well as the dogs, which ran free in the longhouse, and the smoke, which was so thick it could cause blindness. When the Iroquois smoked fish over the fires, Europeans who were new to the experience could not stand to be inside. Samuel de Champlain wrote the following description of an Iroquois longhouse in 1616, as excerpted in Dean R. Snow's *The Iroquois*.

"[The Iroquois' cabins] are in the shape of tunnels or arbors, and are covered with the bark of trees. They are from twenty-five to thirty fathoms long . . . having a passage-way through the middle . . . which extends from one end to the other. On the sides there is a kind of bench, four feet high, where they sleep in summer, in order to avoid the annoyance of the fleas, of which there were great numbers. In winter they sleep on the ground on mats near the fire, so as to be warmer than they would be on the platform. They lay up a stock of dry wood . . . to burn in winter. At the extremity of the cabins there is a space, where they preserve their Indian corn, which they put into great casks made of the bark of trees. . . . They have pieces of wood suspended, on which they put their clothes, provisions, and other things, for fear of the mice, of which there are great numbers. In one of these cabins there may be twelve fires, and twenty-four families. It smokes excessively, from which it follows that many receive serious injury to the eyes, so that they lose their sight towards the close of life. There is no window nor any opening, except that in the upper part of their cabins for the smoke to escape."

The Three Sisters

By the mid–fifteenth century, the culture of the Iroquois revolved around the agricultural products they planted. Especially important were corn, beans, and squash, which they called the "Three Sisters." Anthropologists believe that the Iroquois may have brought seeds of these crops with them when they migrated to the Northeast, but the Iroquois believed they were gifts from their Creator. By the sixteenth century, the Iroquois had cultivated many varieties of all three of these crops. With such a reliable food supply, the Iroquois were less nomadic than the many Native American nations that depended on hunting and gathering.

Iroquois women were responsible for tending the fields, which were divided into family plots. They planted presoaked seeds of Indian corn, or maize, in small hills of dirt about three feet apart. When the maize began to grow, they added beans, which climbed the stalks, and squash, which spread out between the hills and helped to kill weeds. The three products thus supported one another as they grew. Planting them in the same fields also made harvesting easier.

Iroquois women kept their children with them as they worked in the field. Children of all ages would help their mothers and play amid the crops. Babies were carried on cradleboards, which were hung from a tree so that they could watch the women as they worked. Mary Jemison, a white woman who was captured by the Seneca as a child, described the women's work:

> Our labor was not severe. Notwithstanding the Indian women have all the fuel and bread to procure, and the cooking to perform, their task is probably not harder than that of white women, who have those articles provided for them; and their cares certainly are not half as numerous, nor as great. In the summer season, we planted, tended, and harvested our corn, and generally had all of our children with us; but had no master to oversee or drive us, so that we could work as leisurely as we pleased.[8]

Men helped only with the heaviest work. Their main role in the agricultural life of the village was to clear the fields—slow, grueling work that sometimes took several years. The Iroquois used the fields until the soil was depleted of nutrients and no longer yielded adequate quantities of crops. Then, the men would find other fertile land to be cleared. Once these new fields were ready, the entire village would move. Thus, most new villages were located only a few miles from the old ones, so that men would not have to travel far to clear new fields.

An Agricultural Lifestyle

Cultivation furnished villages with a stable source of food that could be stored through the winter. As a hedge against bad weather or other crop damage, the Iroquois would try to harvest enough food to last for two or three years. Usually the harvest was stowed away in communal storehouses and was shared at mealtime with any guests who happened to be present.

The cultivated corn, beans, and squash provided a balanced and varied diet, making up as much as three-quarters of the food supply in some villages. All three products could be boiled, roasted, or baked in various ways.

The Iroquois supplemented their diet with the bounty of the forests around them. During the summer, women and children gathered roots, greens, nuts, and berries to be stored for use during the harsh winter. In the spring, they drained sap from maple trees and boiled it to make maple syrup, which was used to sweeten cornmeal and other foods. Plants and herbs that could be used for medicinal purposes were also collected.

The Hunt Is On

As the women and young children tended the fields and combed the forests for edible plants and berries, the men hunted and fished. Their primary quarry was the deer. Single hunters pursued deer with a bow and arrow or caught them in snares, but deer hunting was more successful when the Iroquois worked together. Small groups of hunters would form a V-shaped line and make loud noises, driving the deer into triangular camouflaged enclosures. Once or twice a year, the Iroquois would hold more elaborate drives that enlisted hundreds of villagers. The hunters' long V could steer many deer toward a river or ravine where others waited with bows and arrows or spears.

Following a hunt, the Iroquois cooked and ate the venison immediately or dried it for the winter. They used the antlers and bones for arrow shafts and tools, the sinew and guts for thread and string, and the hooves for rattles. Also important to the Iroquois were the hides, which were used for kilts, leggings, and skirts.

Although an exhausting and often dangerous activity, bear hunts also were organized regularly. Bear meat was served during religious ceremonies, and bear hides made wonderful blankets. Another favorite prey was the porcupine, whose meat the Iroquois considered a delicacy. Iroquois women cleaned and dyed the quills of the porcupines and used them to decorate clothes, boxes, and jewelry. The Iroquois also fed on the abundant supply of wild turkey in their midst, as well as migratory game birds such as ducks, Canadian geese, and the now-extinct passenger pigeon that passed through their territory.

The Iroquois also hunted smaller animals, including muskrat and beaver. They ate their meat after skinning them for their valuable pelts. The Iroquois preferred to wait until the winter months to catch these animals because their fur was thicker. During the seventeenth and eighteenth centuries, the hunt for beaver would intensify as European traders clamored for more and more beaver pelts to make the fancy hats that were in vogue in Europe.

Even more than hunting, the Iroquois relied on fishing to supplement their diet. The rivers and streams that crisscrossed Iroquois

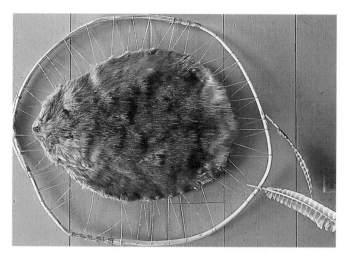

Beaver pelts were a valuable trade item for the Iroquois.

☀ Iroquois Pottery

The Iroquois learned the art of making pottery from the Indians to their south. Women gathered clay from riverbanks, soaked and kneaded it, formed the shape of the pot they wanted, and then fired it to make it hard. The following description of Iroquois pottery is from Ruth M. Underhill's *Red Man's America*.

"Pottery cooking utensils were made by the Iroquois women. In late pre-Columbian and early historic times pottery-making was widely distributed and skillfully accomplished. After the increase of white contacts and trade the craft decreased and was replaced by brass and iron kettles from Europe.

Characteristic Iroquois pots had globular bodies with round bottoms, constricted necks, and straight rims. The latter were usually topped by projecting collars, which were ornamented with incised geometric designs in line-filled triangular plats and chevrons. . . . These collars were often four-sided with an upward turn at each corner. The designs were incised with a sharp instrument (probably of bone) when the clay was still plastic. Other methods of decoration were by indentation, appliqué, and scallops.

The pottery was built up by the coiling process and smoothed by a paddle. After the pot was sun-dried, it was fired in smothered hot coals. The surface . . . was usually smooth and the clay color was gray."

country teemed with a variety of fish, including trout, bass, whitefish, and perch. Throughout the year, groups of men went on fishing trips sometimes lasting for a month or longer. In the spring they netted or speared salmon and shad heading upstream to spawn. When waterways froze over in the winter, they made holes in the ice and dropped nets or fishing lines into the water. Fish that was not consumed immediately was smoked and stored in bark containers.

A People at War

In addition to hunting, the main occupation of Iroquois men was war. Like many of the Indians who lived nearby, the Iroquois believed that the death of a loved one needed to be avenged before the dead could rest in peace. This belief contributed to a bloody cycle of intertribal warfare. Furthermore, courage in battle was one of the main ways a man could prove himself and gain power and prestige. War was simply a fact of life.

The war tactics of the Iroquois were no different than those of their neighbors and depended largely on the element of surprise. A Jesuit once wrote that the Iroquois "approach like foxes, fight like lions and disappear like birds."[9] They fought only during the day, however, because they believed that the sun liked to see their courage. In battle the Iroquois wore armor made from slatted wood to fend off arrows.

The Iroquois were known as fierce warriors—the Mohawk particularly so. One European witness writes that when a Mohawk was spotted on the horizon, the New England Algonquian "fled like sheep before wolves, without attempting to make the least resistance."[10] This was perhaps an overstatement. The Algonquian and other Native American neighbors withstood battles with the Mohawk and other Iroquois tribes for many centuries.

One of the goals of warfare was to take captives. Captured males were forced to run naked through a gauntlet of whips and clubs. If the Iroquois deemed that a captive showed sufficient courage, he was treated with respect and kindness. If not, he was tortured. Sometimes, a captive would be tortured for one or more days, at the end of which his body provided a feast for all. Anthropologist Ruth M. Underhill offers one possible explanation for this harsh practice:

Plainly the basis of the procedure was a sacrificial rite. Yet students of the Indian have suggested that this . . . was a necessary emotional release for people whose daily life was held down to an irksome cooperation. One can imagine that the highly organized Iroquois needed such a relief even more than their neighbors.

. . . Their mere living conditions, by which fifty persons might be crowded into a single dwelling, would be cause enough for a nervous breakdown.[11]

Of course, this twentieth-century viewpoint may not echo the feelings of the Iroquois, who were no doubt more used to living in such close confines.

Adopted by the Iroquois

Many captives were not tortured or killed, however. Women and children were usually spared, and entire villages were adopted after the Iroquois began to lose numbers in the second half of the seventeenth century. In *History of the Five Indian Nations*, written in 1727, historian Cadwallader Colden explains:

It has been [the Iroquois'] constant Maxim . . . to save the Children and Young Men of the People they Conquer, to adopt them into their own Nation, and to educate them as their own Children, without Distinction; These young People soon forget their own Country and Nation; and by this Policy the Five Nations make up the Losses which their Nation suffers by the People they lose in War.[12]

Once adopted, newcomers were treated like members of the family. Mary Jemison explains that after she was adopted to substitute for a lost child, she was renamed and "was ever considered and treated by them as

The Legacy of Lacrosse

Lacrosse has been a part of the Iroquois culture for centuries. The fierce competition among players helped condition Iroquois men for hunting and war. Early games were often played by hundreds of men, and, in the quest to get the ball in the opponent's net and keep it out of yours, almost anything was allowed—tripping, holding, tackling, or charging. The following description of this quintessentially Iroquois game is from Time-Life Books' *Realm of the Iroquois*.

"Lacrosse, a sport currently played around the world, originated with the Native Americans centuries before the first Europeans arrived in North America. According to Iroquois tradition, the game was an ancient gift from the Creator, a divine contest to be played for his pleasure and propitia-tion. Athletes took to the field to settle communal disputes, to beseech the spirits to send down rain for the spring corn, or to ask for divine help in healing the sick.

Early European explorers were astonished to witness hundreds of players competing on fields that stretched for more than a mile. It was a French missionary who in the 1600s gave the sport its present name, noting the bent sticks used by the Indians resembled a bishop's crook, or crosier.

Popular among many disparate tribes, lacrosse was a special passion of the Iroquois, and it was their version that gave rise to the modern sport. By the mid-1800s, Iroquois teams were playing matches and spreading enthusiasm for the game in Montreal and other parts of Canada, in several cities in the United States, and then in Great Britain. By 1878 lacrosse had reached Australia and New Zealand.

Native American teams were barred in 1880 from international amateur competition because some of them had accepted expense money for their trips. It was not until the 1980s that the Iroquois reentered the global arena. Since that time, all-star Iroquois teams have taken part in the World Games and other international tournaments, proudly playing the sport that has remained, as a great Iroquois player has said, 'ingrained in our culture and our lives.'"

The Iroquois used lacrosse to condition men for hunting and war.

a real sister, the same as though I had been born of their mother."[13] Author June Namias elaborates: "The women of this new family and particularly her Indian mother assured her that she would be accepted and protected. . . . Her sisters and the women of the village taught her their language and the economic skills of planting and caring for skins."[14] Thus instructed, an adopted child was prepared, as well, to absorb Iroquois teachings in spiritual matters.

Depending on the Spirit World

Success in all endeavors—agriculture, hunting, war—depended greatly on environmental conditions. The Iroquois lived close to nature, depending on the plant and animal world for their very survival.

For the Iroquois, nature was a source of power—a power that was beyond human control. As authors Denise Lardner Carmody and John Tully Carmody explain:

Like virtually all other traditional peoples, native Americans of the northeast woodlands were profoundly aware of their neediness. . . . Nature impinged on them directly, and so the vagaries of nature held their attention. They knew that a dozen things could go wrong, as quickly as a flash flood or a fire started by lightning. They knew that if the sun, the rain, the wind, and the earth did not cooperate, their crops could go to ruin in a week. [15]

Ceremonies and dances, like this one honoring the Great Spirit, were important to the Iroquois religion.

This dependence on nature instilled in the Iroquois a great respect for the world around them. They worshiped gods who had made the world and continued to oversee it. They gave thanks for the many gifts of nature. They celebrated when the bounty was plentiful and asked for help when it was not. When they fought, they believed the gods looked down on them with pride and helped decide the outcome of the battle. While administering the medicinal plants they gathered from the forests, they also looked to their gods for help in curing sickness and healing wounds. In short, the close ties between the Iroquois and the land on which they lived led to a deep spirituality.

Chapter 3

Religion and Ritual

As in other cultures, Iroquois children learned about the world around them from their elders. Children gathered around longhouse fires at night to listen to stories about how the earth was formed, how gods should be appeased, how to drive out sickness, and what happened after one died. These stories helped explain the mysteries of the world around them.

From their creation myth, they learned that all things on earth were thought to be possessed of spirits that could help people or hurt them. The Iroquois called the greater power that permeated all of nature "orenda."

The Iroquois believed in the powers of animals and magical beings and in the spirit of the sun, war, and hunting. They acted under the guidance of these spirits in everything they did. At annual festivals throughout the year, the Iroquois gave thanks to the gods for the gifts they were given and expressed their hopes for fertile soil and abundant hunting grounds.

The Story of Creation

According to traditional Iroquois beliefs, their ancestors did not come from Asia— or anywhere else. Rather, they believe that they have lived on the North American continent since time began. Because the Iroquois story of creation has been kept alive only through oral accounts, there are differences among accounts, but the basic narrative remains the same among all Iroquoian tribes.

Storytellers explain that long before there were human beings on earth, there were Sky People. The Sky Chief and his wife, Skywoman, were expecting a baby, but before it was born she fell through a hole in the sky toward earth, which was all water. As Skywoman fell, seabirds flew underneath her and held her aloft. Skywoman was afraid, but the animals came to her and asked what they could do to help. She told them that if they got her some soil, she could plant the roots and plants that she had caught between her fingers as she struggled to hold on to her place in the sky. After many attempts, a muskrat was able to bring mud from the bottom of the sea, and Skywoman placed it in the middle of a turtle's back. Since that time, North America has been known as Turtle Island.

Skywoman gave birth to a baby girl. When the baby girl grew into a woman, she in turn gave birth to twins—one good, the other evil. The evil twin was in such a hurry to be born that he punctured his mother's side and killed her. Skywoman buried her daughter, and from the grave grew the Three Sisters (corn, beans, and squash), as well as tobacco and medicinal plants.

When the twins grew up, they made the other things of the world. The good twin made animals, plants, rivers, and other good things, including human beings. The evil twin made diseases and other bad things. As a result, the world today consists of both good and bad elements in tension. According to anthropologist Ruth M. Underhill, "This conception of a battle between good and evil powers is unusual among Indians but seems indigenous with the Iroquois."[16]

A Sacred Respect

The Iroquois believed that they, like all other creatures of the earth, have a responsibility to look after the world that Skywoman and her ancestors created. They taught their children to have respect for

The Iroquois performed many chants and dances to show their respect for the Creator.

the world around them. As one author explains,

Through their stories the children learned that human beings had a special place on the back of the Great Turtle, but that they must not think that they knew better than their Creator nor try to change things or interfere with nature. They learned they had to look after the land, treat the animals with respect, and use the plants and other resources with care. If they forgot to do these things they would destroy the harmony and balance that was given to the world at its creation.[17]

According to Iroquois belief, the good twin lived in the sky, where he watched over what people did and received their offerings of tobacco and other gifts. The Iroquois demonstrated their respect for their Creator and celebrated their good fortune in festivals throughout the year.

The evil twin also continued his influence in the world, spreading sickness, death, famine, and other catastrophes in villages that did not take precautions against him.

Annual Festivals

The oldest Iroquois ceremony is thought to be the Green Corn Festival. This important event was held in August when the first corn was ready to be harvested. It lasted for several days and featured thanksgiving speeches, dances, feasts, and offerings of tobacco, the smoke of which carried the villagers' message skyward to the Creator. Any babies who had been born since midwinter were named at the Green Corn Festival.

When the maize and other crops had been harvested a month or two later, the Iroquois held another celebration to honor and give thanks for their good fortune. Like the Green Corn Festival, the Harvest Festival lasted for several days.

The Iroquois held several other annual ceremonies in coordination with their planting or gathering, including the Maple Festival, the Planting Ceremony, and the Strawberry Festival. Two other common seasonal festivals included the Sun Festival, which was held when the sun began to heat up the earth in the early spring, and the Thunder Ceremony, held in late spring or summer to rouse the spirits to send down rain.

The most elaborate festival, however, was the Midwinter Festival, which was held when the men returned from their late-fall hunt. This festival often lasted over a week and symbolized a time of cleansing and renewal. Before the festival, villagers cleaned their longhouses and also cleaned their hearts by participating in a public confession. When the festival began, they lit fires in their longhouses, and then went from one house to another to stir one another's fires—a symbol of renewal. The village medicine men, or shamans, also stirred all of the fires. The Midwinter Festival also included feasts, dances, and games, including snow snake, an individual game of skill; lacrosse, a team game; and the bowl game, a game of

During the Midwinter Festival, the Iroquois played many games, including lacrosse.

chance, which was believed to evoke the memory of the contest between the good and evil twins. Any babies born since the Green Corn Festival were named during the Midwinter Festival.

The Importance of Dreams

Dream-guessing was another important element of the Midwinter Festival. According to the Iroquois, people's contact with orenda—the invisible force that flowed through the universe—was through dreams. The Iroquois believed that unfulfilled dreams could bring about harm—personal illness or death, or misfortune for the entire community. Anthropologist Dean R. Snow writes, "The Iroquois put much stock in dreams, and have traditionally maintained a relatively modern view of

their significance. While the Algonquian shamans of New England saw dreams as out-of-body experiences, the Iroquois thought them to be the expressions of suppressed desires."[18] Shamans dreamed more than others, and the higher the rank of the dreamer, the more likely the dream had considerable significance. However, anyone's dream was given credence.

To rid dreams of their power, the Iroquois believed that someone other than the dreamer had to fulfill the suppressed desires expressed through the dream. Thus, dream-guessing was an important ritual. At the Midwinter Festival, the Iroquois purged themselves of their unfulfilled wishes by going from house to house and giving riddles and hints about their dream. Others took turns guessing what they had

Prayers

The Iroquois gave thanks to the spirits and prayed to them for help in living a good life. Today, many historians point out the similarities between the prayers of the Iroquois and Christians. This Thanksgiving Prayer is reprinted from *Through Indian Eyes*, published by Reader's Digest.

"Now we will speak about him, Our Creator. He decided, 'Above the world I have created . . . I will continue to look intently and to listen intently to the earth when people direct their voices at me.'

Let there be gratitude day and night for the happiness he has given us. He loves us, he who in the sky dwells. He gave us the means to set right that which divides us."

The Great Spirit Prayer that follows is reprinted from the webpage of the Tuscarora.

"Oh, Great Spirit, whose voice I hear in the wind,

Whose breath gives life to all the world.

Hear me; I need your strength and wisdom.

Let me walk in beauty, and make my eyes ever behold the red and purple sunset.

Make my hands respect the things you have made and my ears sharp to hear your voice.

Make me wise so that I may understand the things you have taught my people.

Help me to remain calm and strong in the face of all that comes towards me.

Let me learn the lessons you have hidden in every leaf & rock.

Help me seek pure thoughts & act with the intention of helping others.

Help me find compassion without empathy overwhelming me.

I seek strength, not to be greater than my brother, but to fight my greatest enemy—Myself.

Make me always ready to come to you with clean hands and straight eyes.

So when life fades, as the fading sunset, my spirit may come to you without shame."

dreamed for and offering the desired item as a gift. When someone guessed correctly, the dreamer kept the gift. This dream-guessing process might take several days but would be completed before the end of the Midwinter Festival, for the people feared that dreams left unfulfilled at festival's end would cause the dreamer to fall ill, spring to be delayed, or catastrophe to strike the village.

Of course, not all dreams could be easily satisfied. Sometimes, a dream expressed a deep fear or desire that could not be appeased with a gift. In these situations, the village might need to participate in a staged event to relieve the dreamer of his or her burden. For example, one account tells of a man who dreamed he was captured and burned alive by the enemy. In response, his fellow villagers erected a scaffold and enacted a mock execution. This was designed to give the dreamer peace of mind.

Giving Thanks and Sacrifices

Giving thanks was an important part of the Iroquois' ceremonial rites. They gave thanks for each other, to the earth, to the winds, thunderers, sun, moon, and stars, and to the Creator himself. This emphasis on thanksgiving was unique among the Iroquois. "Verbal expression of gratitude was not an Indian custom," writes Underhill, "and in fact few tribes had any words for the purpose. A gift or kind deed was reciprocated by gift or deed, often with nothing said about obligation. Almost everywhere the same attitude was held to-

ward Supernaturals. Firstfruits were honored not by thanks or prayer but by praising them or dancing to imitate them."[19]

Sacrificial offerings were another integral part of Iroquois ceremonies. The smoke of the ceremonial tobacco was thought to carry the prayers of the people directly to the Creator. Men grew tobacco specifically for this purpose by scattering seeds in the spring and drying the tobacco leaves over the fire in the fall. The dried tobacco was then stored in communal caches until it was needed for ceremonial purposes. Marine beads, cornmeal, or other valuables might also be offered to appease the gods. In addition, early accounts of Iroquois rituals tell of the sacrifice of a small white dog raised for this purpose.

Both men and women participated fully in public ceremonies. In conjunction with their role as the cultivators of crops, women took a particularly active role in planting ceremonies. As Underhill explains, the Iroquois believed that women's power of fertility was needed for the plants:

A woman could work magic by walking around the cornfield at night, dragging her garments over the ground. The women planters had dances for the corn, beans, and squash, which were spirits, "our supporters," and also for the wild fruits. . . . Honors to the food spirits were paid regularly throughout the season, interspersed with curing rites and social dances.[20]

Medicine Societies

Medicine societies were groups of people who helped others gain power and health, usually by invoking spirits. Ritualistic behavior of the societies often included handling hot coals or blowing ashes, as well as reciting incantations and engaging in ritualistic dances.

There were at least eight medicine societies in Iroquois tribes at the time of European conquest. The best known is perhaps the False Face Society. Some experts believe that the False Face Society came into being as late as the seventeenth century, in order to combat the epidemics that were ravaging Iroquois villages. Both men and women could be members of the False Face Society, but only men engaged in the ritualistic dances.

An Iroquois medicine man from the False Face Society.

The Husk Faces were another group that wore masks. Their masks were made of corn husks and represented spirits of the fields. The Husk Face Society came together to stimulate success in agriculture. The Towii'sas Society, made up solely of women, also focused on agriculture. Its role was to honor corn, beans, and squash—"our supporters." Both the Husk Face and the Towii'sas Societies might also engage in curing ceremonies. The goal of the Little Water Society was to facilitate healing wounds by mixing parts of animals and plants to make medicines. This society was very busy during times of war and met regularly to share successful recipes.

The Shake the Pumpkin Society was the largest of the medicine societies and included most of the members of the other societies. This society engaged in rituals to thank animal helpers who were thought to have pledged their aid in fighting disease and bringing good luck. The Company of Mystic Animals also focused on animal spirits. Its members imitated the animals of their clans. The Iroquois also believed in small fairylike spirits who lived in the forests. The goal of the Little People Society was to maintain good relations with these people, who, like other spirits, could be helpful or mischievous.

Finally, the Ohgiwe Society sponsored ceremonies to honor the dead. Their rituals were thought to help protect the tribe from attacks from the dead. They were also called upon to intervene when people saw ghosts.

Medicine Men

Like any people, the Iroquois had to deal with sickness and death. Iroquois healers were remarkably knowledgeable about the medicinal powers of the many plants found in the forests around them. "Hundreds of plant species were used as medicines according to specific recipes," explains Dean R. Snow. "While many apparently provided only psychological comfort, some had real biochemical value. The sap of the touch-me-not was used to treat poison ivy, and snakeroot leaves were an instant poultice for bee stings."[21] The Iroquois who practiced medicine also were very skillful in setting broken bones and attending to wounds.

Medicine societies were an important aspect of the healing process and religious practice. The Iroquois believed that dreams, witchcraft, or evil spirits could cause physical illness. Thus, some Iroquois medicine societies focused on healing through medicinal recipes, while others focused on the spiritual aspects of healing, attempting to drive out malevolent influences through spells or incantations.

Perhaps the most famous of the Iroquois medicine societies was the False Face Society. The medicine men of this society used wooden masks

that represented the spirit beings who had power to heal. The masks were carved on the trunk of a living tree, which the Iroquois believed would help capture the life-giving spirit within it. They were then painted black, if carved after noon, or red, if carved in the morning. Strands of vegetable fibers and horsehair were used as

Medicine men of the False Face Society believed they could capture the life-giving spirit within trees by carving masks on them.

Increasing the Dosage

The Iroquois believed that illness was caused by an irregularity in the system and used any means deemed necessary to drive out the evil spirits believed to have caused the illness. Theorists speculate that the rapid spread of deadly diseases after European contact caused an increase in the intensity of the medicine men's activities. The curing rituals must have seemed very strange to the Europeans who witnessed them. The following accounts of two different healing rituals were both recorded by the Dutch traveler Harmen van den Bogaert in the 1630s. The first describes an event that took place in a Mohawk village, the second in an Oneida village. Both excerpts are taken from Dean R. Snow's *The Iroquois.*

"Since it was Sunday I looked in on a person who was sick. He had invited into his house two of their doctors who were supposed to heal him. . . . As soon as they arrived, they began to sing, and kindled a large fire, sealing the house all around so that no draft could enter. Then both of them put a snake skin around their heads and washed their hands and faces. They then took the sick person and laid him before the large fire. Taking a bucket of water in which they had put some medicine, they washed a stick in it [and] stuck it down their throats so that the end could not be seen, and vomited on the patient's head and all over his body. Then they performed many [antics] with shouting and rapid clapping of hands, as is their custom, with much display."

• • • • •

"The floor of the house was completely covered with tree bark over which the devil-hunters were to walk. They were mostly old men who were all colored or painted with red paint on their faces because they were to perform something strange. Three of them had garlands around their heads upon which were five white crosses. These garlands were made of deer's hair which they dyed with the roots of herbs. In the middle of this house was a very sick person who had been languishing for a long time, and there sat an old woman who had an empty turtle shell in her hands, in which were beads that rattled while she sang. Here they intended to catch the devil and trample him to death, for they stomped all the bark in the house to pieces, so that none remained whole. Wherever there was but a little dust on the corn, they beat at it with great excitement, and then they blew that dust toward one another and were so afraid that each did his best to flee as if he had seen the devil. After much stomping and running, one of them went to the sick person and took an otter from his hand, and for a long time sucked on the sick man's neck and back. Then he spat in the otter and threw it on the ground, running away with great excitement. Other men then ran to the otter and performed such antics that it was a wonder to see; indeed, they threw fire, ate fire, and threw around hot ashes and embers in such a way that I ran out of the house."

hair. Although the False Face Society consisted of both men and women who had been cured, only men wore the masks or engaged in direct curing of the patient.

Iroquois shamans sprinkled tobacco to expel the evil and engaged in ritualistic dances to call on healing spirits. Conjurers, as the Europeans later called them, also recited incantations, sang ritual songs, and/or blew and sucked over the patient's body. Often, they would produce a small piece of wood or other object that had presumably been drawn from the body, declaring the person healed.

Like other peoples, the Iroquois were respectful of death when it claimed one of their number. Relatives covered their faces and clothing with ashes to represent their grief. The dead were dressed in traditional clothing and buried with food and other necessities for their journey to the other side. Usually the body was buried on the third day after death, but the funeral of someone important would last longer to allow people at some distance to be present. The soul was thought to linger until the tenth day after death. On the tenth day, a feast featuring the favorite foods of the deceased was held to celebrate his or her departure. A year later, the Iroquois held another feast to mark the end of the mourning period. General Feasts of the Dead were also held once or twice a year to remember all those who had died.

Religion and Politics

For the Iroquois, religion was closely tied to the ways in which they lived. Their closeness to nature had given them a great reverence for the world around them and the invisible spirits were present everywhere. Their religious practices also helped them forge ties with others in the village. The many annual festivals allowed them time to celebrate—to dance, to feast, to play games. Perhaps more important, it was an opportunity to reconfirm their willingness to help one another, both as individuals and as a group, since mutual assistance was essential to their survival.

But religion was not the Iroquois' only method of reaffirming a sense of community. They also had a highly complex political structure. In many ways, religion and politics went hand in hand. For example, the organizational rules by which the Iroquois lived ensured that the dead and those who mourned them were properly cared for, that witches who spread evil were executed, and that children were brought up to respect the beliefs and traditions by which the people lived.

Chapter 4

Political and Social Organization

Though relatively few in number, the Iroquois were able to draw strength from the alliances they forged, both within their villages and with one another. The political organization of the village helped enable the Iroquois to live in small, close communities and encouraged the formation of the tight bonds needed to succeed. As one historian writes, "Fierce conquerors though they were toward outsiders, the Iroquois spoke constantly about love and peace among themselves. And they needed these things if their little communities were to survive."[22]

The political system of the Iroquois was highly democratic. All meetings were open to anyone who wanted to attend, and decisions were made by consensus. As a result, skills of diplomacy and persuasion were cherished. The men selected to lead their clans, villages, and nations were expected to lead by example and wisdom.

Well before the first European contact, the five nations that have come to be known as the Iroquois consolidated their power by forming a loose confederation. The defined purpose of the confederacy was to forge peace. Council chiefs met regularly to reinforce the code of peace and make plans that would affect all of the five member nations. The Iroquois' highly organized, democratic political structure enabled them to become a dominant force in their area in the seventeenth century.

The Family

At the core of the Iroquois individual's life was a close-knit family. Careful family planning was important to the Iroquois because women who were responsible for farming could not also take care of several small children. As Dean R. Snow writes, "A child born too soon after an older sibling had little chance of survival. An unwanted child would not be kept long, but once accepted children were loved beyond all else."[23] Families would promptly try to replace a child who died, either through pregnancy or adoption.

As a result of family planning, nuclear families were small—three children spaced well apart was considered the ideal. However, extended families were closer than in most other societies. A family was not simply mother, father, and siblings, but also included grandparents, aunts, uncles, cousins, and in-laws. In fact, before the sixteenth century, Iroquois children called their aunts by the same word they used for their biological mothers.

Extended family members lived in the same village, usually under the same roof, and were only separated upon marriage.

The Importance of Wampum

The Iroquois used wampum belts to record treaties and other main events. Some belts would take several years to make and required considerable expertise to decipher. The following excerpt from *Realm of the Iroquois*, a Time-Life book, describes the use of wampum.

"Wampum, tiny beads fashioned from seashells, played a major role in Iroquois life. Woven into belts and other articles, wampum served as a currency during the heyday of the fur trade, but its value to the Iroquois and neighboring tribes was more spiritual than monetary. Wampum, in reality, evoked the very founding of the Iroquois confederacy. According to legend, the Onondaga chief Hiawatha, mourning the deaths of his wife and daughters, met the prophet Deganawida, who consoled the grieving man with strings of white shells. (The word wampum is derived from an Algonquian phrase meaning 'strings of white.') The two men, bonded in friendship, worked together to forge the league of tribes.

Possessing a rich oral tradition but no written alphabet, the Iroquois used the beads as memory aids to record tribal history and sacred pacts. They first traded for wampum with coastal tribes, who used conch and quahog shells to craft the white beads, signifying purity, and the purple ones, which stood for grief. White beads reddened with ocher symbolized war. The belt's design also held a message: A row of diamonds, for example, might mean friendship, while squares might signify council fires. The information conveyed by the colors and designs of wampum documents was memorized by tribal wampum keepers, or historians.

Wampum was also essential to diplomacy between the Iroquois and the Europeans. Before treaty talks, the Iroquois exchanged wampum as a sign of sincerity. When a pact was made, its terms were woven into a belt, and the agreement was sealed by a gift of wampum. Although many wampum objects are now possessed by non-Indian collectors and museums, the Iroquois have begun to reclaim this vital part of their heritage by successfully negotiating the return of a host of items, including more than two dozen belts."

Marriages were often arranged by families and bound together not just husband and wife, but in-laws as well.

Extended family played an intimate role in raising children. Children learned from their elder relatives everything they needed to know about life as an Iroquois, including the ancient stories that explained why the world was as it was. Young girls were trained in the traditional ways of women; young boys were taught to be hunters and warriors. Above all, children were taught to have respect for their elders. The Iroquois used criticism and peer pressure rather than corporal punishment to discipline their children.

Names had great symbolism for the Iroquois. Babies were named during the Green Corn and the Midwinter Festivals. Parents (usually mothers) selected a baby's name from a list of names reserved for the clan into which the baby was born and that were not in use. When the child reached adulthood, he or she sometimes was given a new name. Often, this new name pointed to an existing or desired personality trait that suited the individual.

The Extended Family: The Longhouse and Clan

The longhouse served as a major form of organization of the Iroquois villages and

The longhouse housed extended families and served as an important political unit within the village.

Iroquois clans represented a larger family unit and helped forge ties within the village. Some of the symbols for Iroquois clans were the Bear, Wolf, Turtle, Deer, and Beaver.

brought families into larger alliances. "In the world of the Iroquois," writes one historian, "nothing expressed the idea of community more than the longhouse. Just as the nations of the Iroquois League lived geographically lined in union, so did Iroquois families dwell side by side in longhouses."[24] Young people came to rely on their relatives in the longhouse for advice and mentoring. The oldest and most respected woman of the longhouse, known as the clan mother, presided over the longhouse and its ceremonies and selected the men to represent the longhouse within the village.

Clans were formed from several longhouses and represented a larger family unit. All the people of a clan claimed descent from a common ancestor, although they were often related more in notion than in reality. According to what is known as a matrilineal system, they traced their lineage on their mother's side of the family. At birth, a person became a member of his or her mother's clan. Property was owned by the women in the clan and was passed down through the mother.

People were not allowed to marry others in the same clan. Although much has been written about the marriage taboo within clans, Dean R. Snow argues that the "regulation of marriage was not the primary function of clans." He suggests a more important purpose: "Clans probably arose to facilitate trade and exchange between residential groups. . . . A clan identification provided fictive [assumed] kinship for men traveling away from home; a turtle was always welcome in the home of another turtle, regardless of distance and language barriers."[25] Thus, clans served a valuable purpose in forging ties among villages and allowed the Iroquois tribes to extend their hunting grounds far from home.

Each clan claimed a bird or animal as its name and symbol. The number of clans varied from one nation to another. The Mohawk and Oneida had three clans: Turtle, Wolf, and Bear. The Onondagas, Cayugas, and Senecas added to these three the Snipe, Heron, Beaver, Deer, Eel, and Hawk.

Moieties

In each village, the clans were divided into two groups, called moieties. Members of

Hiawatha: Myth or History?

Because it has been passed down orally from one generation to the next, the story of Hiawatha (also called Hayenwatha) varies from tribe to tribe and village to village, but throughout the six nations he is treated as a cultural icon.

Some historians believe that Hiawatha was in fact not one person, but rather a composite of two or more people from the Iroquoian tribes who worked to form the Iroquois confederacy. These people believe that the description of Hiawatha represents the best qualities of each person. Others argue that Hiawatha was a real person, accurately depicted in the Iroquois legend that

Henry Wadsworth Longfellow's The Song of Hiawatha *tells the tale not of Hiawatha but of Nanabozho.*

exists to this day. Additional confusion about Hiawatha stems from the use of his name by the poet Henry Wadsworth Longfellow in *The Song of Hiawatha*, a poem written in 1855. This poem actually tells the tale not of Hiawatha but of Nanabozho, an Algonquian mythic hero whose tale is somewhat similar to Hiawatha's.

Nor is there consensus about when Hiawatha lived. Experts know that the Iroquois confederacy for which he is credited existed by the mid-1500s, and many believe it was formed well before this time. Because the Iroquois did not read or write, the only existing documentary evidence of the formation of the confederacy is a wampum belt. Sometimes called Hiawatha's Belt, this was composed of five figures. In the center is a great pine tree under which the Iroquois met in council. On either side of the central device are two squares connected to each other and to the tree by a narrow band. These represent the five original tribes. The symbols of the wampum belt are now used as a flag for the Iroquois confederacy.

After the formation of the Iroquois confederacy, Hiawatha held a position of great importance. He was given the leadership position of Keeper of the Wampum. As such, he was responsible for keeping the wampum belts that represented the Law of Great Peace and important agreements made thereafter by the League of Five Nations.

each moiety were required to marry someone from the other moiety. Moieties also squared off against each other in ceremonial games, such as the bowl game. But perhaps the most important function of moieties was the condolence and funeral services members provided for one another. Immediately following a death, the members of the moiety of the deceased immediately assumed the role of the grieving party, while members of the other moiety consoled them and took over arrangements for burial. As Dean R. Snow explains:

> The elaborate funeral rite ensured that everyone was either grieving or condoling, and that no one could be blamed for causing the death. The process effectively shifted blame outside the close-knit immediate community, whether it comprised one village or several allied villages. It also unified the rage of the survivors, and turned grief into grievance against unknown and unknowing perpetrators elsewhere.[26]

Like other Iroquois customs, the moieties helped minimize conflict within the village or closely aligned villages.

Village Leadership

Each clan in a village appointed its own chiefs, who were responsible for speaking for the clan at village councils. The chiefs

Iroquois leaders were always men from the same family and were usually chosen for their hunting skills, courage in battle, or ability to influence others.

were always men and always came from the same families, which the Iroquois today speak of as "noble" families. Succession was not automatic, however. Iroquois leaders were usually chosen because of hunting skills, courage in battle, or ability to influence others. Some leaders were medicine men who had proven ability to cure the sick.

The chiefs were expected to rule by leadership and wisdom. Carol Jacobs, a Cayuga Bear Clan Mother, writes:

> In making any law, our chiefs must always consider three things: the effect of their decision on peace; the effect on the natural world; and the effect on seven generations in the future. We believe that all law makers should be required to think this way, [and] that all constitutions should contain these rules.[27]

The Iroquois had separate war and civil councils. War councils were called to initiate raids or to defend against enemy encroachment, but civil councils met regularly to discuss events that affected all concerned, commemorate deaths of prominent people, and plan joint activities. Village chiefs also settled disputes within the village and made other decisions that affected the entire community, such as whether to build a new longhouse. Because the Iroquois lived in such close quarters, maintaining unity was an important part of the council's responsibilities.

Women and Politics

Women played an important role in Iroquois political life. They nominated clan chiefs and had the power to remove them from office. Women also played an important advisory role. As one French missionary observed, women "were always the first to deliberate on private and community matters. They hold their councils apart and, as a result of their decisions, advise the chiefs."[28]

The influence of women—and the women themselves—stayed in the village, however. As anthropologist Nancy Bonvillain explains, "the strength of the League and of the women in it also depended on its local character. That is, although intertribal meetings were held and were occasions of great importance and solemnity, decisions were made and approved on a local basis, thus allowing for the influence of women, who tended to remain in the villages."[29] Only men attended intertribal council meetings, negotiated treaties, or spoke on behalf of the village.

Iroquois Rule

The Iroquois did not rule through proclamations or laws. Instead they tried to resolve disputes and make decisions by reaching consensus, rather than by majority rule. All meetings were open to anyone wanting to attend, and everyone had a chance to speak on issues. "Among the Haudenosaunee participatory democracy meant that on some level every individual had a right to voice an opinion and to agree or disagree on actions to be taken,"[30] explains Oren Lyons, an Onondaga chief.

There were no police or jails in Iroquois villages. This did not mean, however, that there was no punishment for wrongdoing. A person guilty of theft or causing injury to another usually had to compensate the victim by giving him or her furs or other valuables. Murder also required the murderer and his or her family to provide the

Benjamin Franklin's Impressions

Benjamin Franklin was considered to be an "Indian buff." Some scholars believe his knowledge of the Iroquois confederacy was incorporated into the Plan of Union he presented in 1754 at a conference in Albany. Here, Franklin shares some of his observations about Indians. This excerpt is taken from Robert W. Venables' essay "American Indian Influences on the America of the Founding Fathers," in *Exiled in the Land of the Free.*

"The Indian Men, when young, are Hunters and Warriors; when old, Counsellors; for all their Government is by the Counsel or Advice of the Sages; there is no Force, there are no Prisons, no Officers to compel Obedience, or inflict Punishment. Hence they generally study Oratory; the best Speaker having the most influence.

Benjamin Franklin.

The Indian Women till the Ground, dress the Food, nurse and bring up the children, and preserve and hand down to Posterity the Memory of Public Transactions. . . .

Having frequent Occasions to hold public Councils, they have acquired great Order and Decency in conducting them. The old Men sit in the foremost Ranks, the Warriors in the next, and the Women and Children in the hindmost. The Business of the Women is to take exact notice of what passes, imprint it in their Memories, for they have no writing, and communicate it to their Children. They are the Records of the Council, and they preserve Tradition of the Stipulations in Treaties a hundred Years back, which when we compare with our Writings we always find exact. He that would speak, rises. The rest observe a profound Silence. When he has finished and sits down, they leave him five or six Minutes to recollect, that if he has omitted any thing he intended to say, or has any thing to add, he may rise again and deliver it. To interrupt another, even in common Conversation, is reckoned highly indecent. How different it is from the Conduct of a polite British House of Commons, where scarce a Day passes without some Confusion that makes the Speaker [of the House] hoarse in calling to order; and how different from the mode of Conversation in many polite Companies of Europe, where if you do not deliver your Sentence with great Rapidity, you are cut off in the middle of it."

family of the deceased with extravagant gifts. This was designed to help Iroquois families avenge the death of their loved ones at the hands of others within the village. Revenge for the murder of a family member by someone from another village, however, was one of the main reasons for the ongoing warfare among villages.

The punishment for more serious offenses, including treason and witchcraft, was usually death. The village elders decided whether accusations of witchcraft were true, taking the character of the accused into consideration. Those convicted usually had a record of selfish or disruptive behavior.

A Confederation Is Formed

According to legend, two men—Deganawidah (also called Dekanawida), a Huron, and Hiawatha (also called Hayenwatha), an Onondaga—grew tired of the intertribal warfare that raged in an unending series of attempts to avenge the loss of loved ones. In their desire to establish lasting peace, they proposed forming a family of tribes that would agree to stop fighting. The clan chiefs would become the chiefs of the confederacy, but the clans and tribes would not lose their independence.

Deganawidah and Hiawatha carried their message to the other tribes living in the area, asking them to consider joining in an alliance of peace. Hiawatha told the chiefs, "Carry no anger and hold no grudges. Think of continuing generations of our families, think of our grandchildren and of those yet unborn."[31]

The Mohawk were the first to agree to confederation, and the Oneida soon followed suit. Before long, the Cayuga and Seneca also joined the confederacy. Although historians are unsure when the so-called League of Five Nations was formed, there is evidence that it was in place by the mid–sixteenth century.

The Great Law of Peace

The government of the Five Nations was based on written law. To record this law, the Iroquois did not use pen and paper. Instead, they strung together shells and shell beads called wampum. According to Iroquois legend, Hiawatha created wampum, but archaeological evidence indicates that it existed long before Hiawatha's birth.

The main statute of the league was the Kainerekawa, or Great Law of Peace, which simply stated that members of the five participating nations should not engage in war with one another. Oren Lyons writes that the league

> is the earliest surviving governmental tradition in the world that we know of based on the principle of peace; it was a system that provided for peaceful succession of leadership; it served as a kind of early United Nations; and it installed in government the idea of accountability to future life and responsibility.[32]

Although the tribes continued to manage internal affairs independently, they dealt with other tribes, and later with foreign powers, as one entity. This made it

A Mohawk man and his son attend a ceremony. The Mohawk was the first Iroquois tribe to join the League of Five Nations.

easier for the Iroquois to combine forces against external foes. In fact, according to the law, alien peoples who were not willing to accept peace were automatically assumed to be enemies:

> When the council of the League has for its object the establishment of the Great Peace among the people of an outside nation and that nation refuses to accept the Great Peace, then by such refusal they bring a declaration of war upon themselves from the Five Nations. Then shall the Five Nations seek to establish the Great Peace by a conquest of the rebellious nation.[33]

For decades to come, the Iroquois would test their strength against their neighbors, taking them by conquest and building what some historians have called the "Iroquois Empire."

Governance of the Five Nations

The Iroquois confederacy established ceremonies and conventions that helped preserve the peace among the five nations. It was governed by representatives from each of the five nations—the Onondaga had fourteen representatives, the Cayuga ten, the Oneida and Mohawk each had nine, and the Seneca had eight. Of these fifty places on the council, one was always left empty—it was felt that Hiawatha's place could not be filled by anyone else.

These league representatives met at least once a year, usually in late summer, at the council fire in Onondaga territory. A French missionary wrote, "There all the deputies from the different nations are present to make their complaints and receive the necessary satisfaction in mutual gifts, by means of which they maintain a good understanding with one another."[34] The annual meetings provided an important opportunity for all nations to reconfirm their peace compact and discuss issues that affected all of the member nations.

Each of the five tribes had a single vote, and all were considered brothers. There was, however, a sort of pecking order among the tribes: the Onondaga, Mohawk, and Seneca were called Elder Brothers; the Oneida and Cayuga were the Younger Brothers.

As in Iroquois villages, the confederation's decisions were not made by majority rule; instead, all decisions of the council had to be unanimous and were reached by consensus and compromise.

This sometimes required a long debate, and meetings often lasted for many days.

The council's decisions did not bind the individual nations to act. Instead,

> Any proposal brought to the Haudenosaunee was carried to each of the nations, where it was discussed in either clan or general meetings; the sentiments of the nation were then carried by the principal chiefs to the confederate council, known as the Grand Council. The ancient custom that established the council also delegated to the council the power to act in the interest of all the confederated nations, and the chiefs had the authority to negotiate details of a proposed agreement according to their own judgment and in line with political reality.[35]

Working together, the Iroquois posed a formidable adversary, not only for neighboring Native American nations, but also for the French, Dutch, and English who lived nearby and traded with their enemies. By the mid–seventeenth century, the Iroquois were a dominant force among the Native Americans. However, the loose alliance among the Iroquois would not prove strong enough to defend against the encroachment of whites in the centuries to come.

Chapter 5

The Coming of the White Man

The presence of seashells from the Atlantic coast in early Iroquois villages illustrates that trade had been practiced long before European contact. In addition to enabling Indians to acquire otherwise unobtainable items, trade helped the Iroquois forge bonds and maintain friendly relations with other villages. As one historian explains:

> Aside from the clan ties that transcended local boundaries, trade was a time-honored instrument of conciliation. The Iroquoians regarded trade as a test of friendship in which each side honored the other with gifts. Such amicable exchanges often helped potential rivals overcome formidable barriers of language and custom. [36]

The Iroquois considered trade "ritualistic present-giving between groups or peoples at peace with each other." [37] "Peace and trade we take to be one thing," [38] summarized one Seneca. Trade with Europeans, however, was based on economics rather than on peace or relationships, a modification of tradition that would soon change the nature of trade among the northeastern tribes.

Trade in Pre-European America

Before European contact, the Iroquois used tools made from wood, stone, and shells. In 1534, Jacques Cartier led a group of French explorers to the St. Lawrence River and met with the people who lived there. Almost immediately, the Native Americans began to covet European goods, including metal goods, cloth, and glass beads, which "had ancient and widespread magico-religious uses throughout the Great Lakes and Northeastern Woodland areas." [39] In 1634 the Dutchman Harmen van den Bogaert noted that his Iroquois hosts had "good timber axes, French shirts, coats, and razors." [40]

Throughout the next century, the fur trade would have a profound and lethal fertile hunting territories became increasingly aggressive and increasingly deadly. Historian Francis Jennings writes that conflict was inevitable:

> As the trade bound tribe and colony together, it divided tribe from tribe and colony from colony. In that fact lies a tragedy of epic proportions. In their competition to gain advantage in the trade, tribes rejected the impulse to unite against invading colonials, and their strivings were incited further by competing colonials. No feasible way existed in the conditions of that era to prevent the competition from heightening to bloodshed. [41]

Whereas once the Iroquois and other tribes were self-sufficient, before long they became dependent on trade with the white man, craving metal axes, hoes, and knives, and, of course, firearms and ammunition. As explained in *Through Indian Eyes*:

> As the people grew accustomed to metal tools, they lost the arts of chipping flint into arrowheads and shaping pieces of bone into knives and scrapers. As a result, foreign-made articles that began as luxuries were soon necessities. Without metal farm tools, Indian villagers could not raise

Soon after French explorer Jacques Cartier sailed up the St. Lawrence River, he began trading metal goods, cloth, and glass beads with Native Americans who lived in the area.

effect on the life of the Iroquois and other Indians of the Northeast. Not only did European contact provide Native Americans with far more deadly weapons than they had used previously, but economic viability soon came to depend on the defeat of enemies. As beaver and other animal pelts became scarce due to extensive hunting, competition for enough food to sustain themselves. They were growing dependent on the white traders for their very survival.[42]

Europeans brought not just the items they traded, but also epidemic disease. Thus, in addition to the many hundreds lost to war, northeastern Indians lost even more to disease. No village was spared, and some villages lost half of their population. As sickness took its toll in village after village, capture and adoption became critical to survival.

The Iroquois also lost members to Christianity, and by the end of the century, sizable villages of converts—mostly Mohawk—had been established near Montreal. The first to make a concerted effort were French missionaries who joined Indian villages throughout the region.

The Early Fur Trade

The first recorded direct contact between the Iroquois and Europeans took place in 1609, when French explorer Samuel de Champlain joined forces with Algonquian and Huron—both longtime enemies of the Iroquois. By this time, the Huron had become the French traders' main allies. They obtained pelts from their western Indian neighbors and carried them in canoes along the St. Lawrence River to French trading posts, a route that required them to pass through Iroquois country. For years, the Iroquois had hampered the fur trade along the St. Lawrence River by raiding fur-laden canoes and villages.

When their Indian allies asked the French for help putting an end to Iroquois harassment, the French complied. The Iroquois were unprepared for war against Europeans. Unfamiliar with firearms, they wore traditional wooden armor that could not stop speeding bullets. A bloody battle at Lake Champlain resulted in the death of more than fifty Iroquois, including three Mohawk chiefs. Just a year later, even more Iroquois warriors were killed at the Battle of Richelieu.

This was only the beginning of the intertribal carnage that has become known to historians as the Beaver Wars. For the next seventy years, the Iroquois would fight against neighboring tribes for access to and control over the fur trade.

Going Dutch

Thwarted by the French, the Iroquois began to look to the Dutch, who had settled near present-day Albany, and the English, who had settled in New England. However, several Indian tribes—including the Mahican, Algonquian, and Abenaki—lived between the Iroquois and the European trading sites, causing conflict. The Mahican, whose lands separated Mohawk territory and Dutch trading posts, demanded payment for passage through their territory. After much bloodshed, the Mohawk defeated the Mahican in 1628 to gain access to Fort Orange, which had become the center of the Dutch fur trade.

In clashes with the French, the Iroquois had learned a lesson: Power over one's enemies came with firepower. Thus, they

Missionaries Bear the Good Word

As the French fur traders sought out Indians willing and able to bring them valuable pelts, French missionaries attempted to convert Native Americans to Christianity. The Jesuits who traveled among the Indian villages seeking souls were remarkably successful in their efforts. At the request of the Onondaga, who wanted to curry favor with the French, the Jesuits built a mission in the midst of Onondaga territory in 1654. In 1667 and 1668, a small group of Oneida converts left their home to establish a village near the French settlement of Montreal. Soon, Onondaga, Huron, and especially Mohawk joined the Oneida in the village that came to be called Caughnawaga (which means "at the rapids"). The Caughnawaga Indians became steadfast allies of the French, joining them in battle against the Iroquois and other Native American Nations, as well as against other European forces competing for control over the New World.

The missionaries proved to be a divisive force among the Iroquois. The Iroquois resented the exodus from their ranks of new converts to Christianity. Some villagers blamed the French missionaries for spreading deadly diseases. Conservative Iroquois also were angered by the missionaries' insistence that converts not only abandon but scorn traditional rites and ceremonies.

At Onondaga, the animosity toward the missionary grew, fueled by the escalation of disease. Within two years of its establishment, more than five hundred children and many adults had died. In 1658, just a few years after the mission was built at Onondaga, the Mohawk planned an attack on the mission to destroy it. The Jesuits were forewarned and fled the territory, but the underlying tension among the Iroquois nations remained.

Jesuit missionaries traveled from village to village, successfully converting many Native Americans to Christianity.

In the seventeenth century, the Iroquois escalated their trade relations with the Dutch.

The Dutch extended their friendship with the Mohawk to include the other Iroquois tribes. By this time, however, the Iroquois had depleted the beaver population in their territory. Survival depended on finding another way to obtain the pelts on which they had come to depend.

Smashing the Competition

Meanwhile, the Huron fur trade continued unabated. The Huron were getting richer as the Iroquois got poorer. The Iroquois were further antagonized by the growing alliance between the Huron and the Susquehannock, who lived to their south in what is now Pennsylvania.

The Iroquois had never ceased to raid Huron villages, but their attacks were becoming increasingly devastating. Whereas combat had once consisted of small raids to capture people and furs, the Iroquois now aimed to wipe out villages and kill all inhabitants. In a 1649 attack on a Huron village, a thousand Seneca and Mohawk warriors killed three hundred Huron and burned the village. "This devastation of their own kinsmen marked a turning point in Iroquois history," writes Ruth M. Underhill. "The Five Nations began to send out armies of from five hundred to over a thousand men. Their aim was complete annihilation of tribes handling

stepped up their trade with the Dutch to acquire better guns and more ammunition. A 1643 trade treaty between the Mohawk and the Dutch cemented an alliance that proved to be enduring. The Iroquois and the Dutch called their alliance the Covenant Chain. The metaphor stood for the permanent friendship that both sides agreed could not be broken.

The Fur Trade at Albany

The towns built on the frontier were often surrounded by a wall to protect them from attack. The following description of Albany, the main center of the Dutch and then English fur trade, is reprinted from Douglas Edward Leach, *The Northern Colonial Frontier: 1607–1763.*

"A visitor arriving at Albany by boat in 1680 would see before him a compact settlement sloping from the riverbank up to a palisaded fort. A wall of vertical stakes completely surrounded Albany, reminding the visitor that this area still was frontier territory. Within this protecting wall were some eighty or ninety dwellings and two churches, arranged along the sides of regular streets. A short distance outside the gates, on both sides of the town, stood groups of lodges provided as living quarters for the Indians when they came to Albany to trade their furs. During the summer months, when this trading was at its height, Albany was a busy place, with Indians and traders visiting back and forth, examining bundles of furs and haggling over prices. Below the town, along the riverbank, the ketches and other small river craft waited to take on their cargoes of peltry destined for New York and the markets of Europe. This was the principal fur-trading center of English North America."

the fur trade or else conquest and tribute."[43] Unlike the Dutch, the French sold firearms only to Christian converts—a move made to protect the missionaries living among the Indians. Thus, the Huron were outgunned by their Iroquois neighbors.

In just a few years, the Iroquois accomplished their goal: The once-powerful Huron fled the territory to join neighboring groups, including the Petun, members of the Neutral confederacy, and the Erie. Their control of the fur trade was brought to an end. Still, the Iroquois were not satisfied. Feeling invincible and perhaps fearing that the Huron would take revenge, or

that they might once again gain control of the fur trade, armies of Iroquois invaded the villages of the Petun, Neutral, and Erie. Again they succeeded in forcing these groups farther west, relinquishing vast beaver lands. Conquest over the Susquehannock proved more difficult because they were better armed and their villages were better fortified. In 1675, however, after more than twenty years of bloody battles, they too succumbed to the Iroquois.

The Iroquois were at the peak of their power. They had driven out their Native American adversaries and bolstered their numbers by adopting thousands of captives into their ranks. Whole villages were sometimes incorporated at once into Iroquois villages. An estimated two thousand Huron joined the ranks of the Iroquois between 1648 and 1650—these on top of the hundreds who had been adopted previously. By 1668 two-thirds of the Oneida village were Algonquin and Huron who, according to a Jesuit witness, "have become Iroquois in temper and Inclination."[44]

Extending the Covenant Chain

In 1664 the English conquered Dutch New Netherland and renamed it New York. The Iroquois pounced on the opportunity to ally themselves with their new neighbors, and the fur trade continued with little change.

The English had decreed that all trade was to take place at the British fort at Albany rather than in Indian villages or other places. This measure was designed to protect the traders from raids by other Native Americans and to protect the fur trade from the encroachment of other individuals or colonies. To further secure the fur trade, the new governor of New York issued a proclamation forbidding other English colonies to make treaties with the Indians living within the colony's borders without the sanction of the New York government.

The Iroquois applied their significant diplomatic skills to gain other allies among the British colonies. In 1677 the Five Nations joined in the Covenant Chain with New York, Massachusetts Bay, Connecticut, Maryland, and Virginia. Later, when the Covenant Chain was extended to Pennsylvania, the governor outlined "some of the Motives for cultivating a good Understanding" with the Indians:

> These Indians by their situation are a Frontier to some of [the English colonies], and from thence, if Friends, are Capable of Defending their Settlements; If Enemies, of making Cruel Ravages upon them; If Neuters, they may deny the French

In 1664, the Dutch governor surrendered New Netherland to the English.

a Passage through their Country, and give us timely notice of their designs.[45]

"For their part," writes historian Alan Axelrod, "the Iroquois used the [chain] as the means of consolidating their own power and influence."[46]

Having gained European allies, the Iroquois turned their attention to coordinating the Native American nations. The Covenant Chain was extended to the Mahican and Delaware, and later to other tribes as well. The chain gave the Iroquois the authority to represent its members during negotiations.

The Covenant Chain brought the Iroquois into strong alliance with the English colonies and formerly hostile Indian groups to their south and east, thereby securing those borders. In the decades to come, other colonies replaced New York as the primary power of the Covenant Chain, and the English government took charge directly in 1755, but the position of the Iroquois league at the chain's center remained unchallenged.

French Frustration and Retaliation

The Iroquois had not managed to gain a monopoly over the fur trade to their north, however. The Ottawa Indians who lived on the shores of Lake Huron took over where the Huron had left off. But by the second half of the seventeenth century, the commercial center of the fur trade had shifted to Fort Orange, which had been renamed Fort Beverwyck. The Dutch traders who continued to live there under English rule paid more (in terms of firearms, ammunition, cloth, and other goods) than the French. As historian Douglas Edward Leach explains:

This prevailing price advantage, caused by more advanced development of English manufacturing industry, English domination of the sea lanes, the high import duties levied on trading goods by the Canadian authorities, and the fact that the St. Lawrence River remained frozen during the long Canadian winters, was to be a major factor in the struggle between England and France for the fur trade of North America. [47]

The French were unable even to control their own people's trading activities. In addition to the many pelts lost to Iroquois raids, they lost furs to French smugglers, called *coureurs de bois*, who had no qualms about bypassing legal trading partners to obtain higher prices paid at Albany.

A Tentative Alliance

Again and again, the Iroquois tried to establish trade with New France. "We are born free," said an Onondaga elder defending the Iroquois' right to establish alliances with whoever benefited them. "We may go where we please, and carry with us whom we please, and buy and sell what we please."[48] But New France saw the Iroquois not as a potential trading partner, but as a troublesome force disrupting their

☀ Ferocious Spirit

War was a way of life among the Indians living in New York. The violence of intertribal warfare escalated as a result of the fur trade. The Iroquois were known for their ferocious spirit, but here we see that the Huron and neighboring groups could be just as vicious. In *Chronicle of the Indian Wars*, Alan Axelrod recounts a 1638 clash between the Huron and the Iroquois.

"Throughout the 1640s and as early as 1638, Huron and Iroquois war parties came to blows in raiding and guerrilla actions ranging from apparently random scalpings to the invasion and burning of villages.

An episode in 1638 illustrates the ferocious spirit of these peoples. A war party of 100 Iroquois met some 300 Hurons and Algonquins. It is a commonplace observation on Indian warfare that one party rarely attacks another unless the attacker enjoys substantial superiority of numbers. Nevertheless, Ononkwaya, an Oneida chief, refused to back down. 'Look!' he is reported to have said, 'the sky is clear; the Sun beholds us. If there were clouds to hide our shame from his sight, we might fly; but, as

it is, we must fight while we can.' All but four or five of the Iroquois warriors were killed or captured—and consigned to death by torture. The execution of Ononkwaya was related by a Jesuit missionary. The chief, unflinching, was roasted on a scaffold. When the Hurons thought him nearly dead, one of his tormentors scalped him— whereupon Ononkwaya leaped up, grabbed some burning brands, and drove the crowd back from the scaffold. They threw sticks, stones, and live coals at him until he finally stumbled. The Hurons seized him and threw him into the fire. But, again, he leaped out, a blazing brand in each hand, and ran toward the town, as if to set it ablaze. His captors tripped him with a long pole and then fell upon him, cutting off his hands and feet. Again, they threw him into the fire, and again he rolled off the pyre, crawling toward the crowd on elbows and knees. His gaze was fearsome enough that, even in his hopeless state, the crowd recoiled—only to rush forward upon him and, at last, cut off his head."

trade. They feared that their own Indian trading allies would join the ever-growing number of groups who were part of the Covenant Chain and traded with the English at Fort Orange. They also were becoming increasingly exasperated with the Iroquois' continued raids on tribes as far

west as Ohio and Illinois and north into Ontario. To protect their trade, the French set up a string of forts along the western border. As a further show of force, the governor of New France led an invading force of more than two thousand French and Indians against the Seneca in June of

1687, destroying Seneca villages and burning their fields.

The alliance between England and the Iroquois nations did little to help the Iroquois' woes with New France. Francis Jennings writes, "[England's] rulers were incompetent novices in Indian affairs, easily diddled by experienced neighbors and not much use to their clients."[49] As France and England began to compete over the conquest of New World lands, the Iroquois were swept up, unwitting participants in the competition played out on North American soil. According to Douglas Edward Leach:

> Even the English king, James II, was becoming aware of the importance of the Five Nations, for he ordered Dongan [New York's governor] to claim them as subjects of the Crown entitled to the protection of English arms. It was the fur trade more than anything else which had lured both the French and the English deep into the wilderness during the seventeenth century. And it was ambition to dominate the fur trade through favorable alliances with important groups of Indians which now was pushing the two rival colonial blocks toward the brink of war.[50]

The battle lines had been drawn. The Iroquois would spend the next century trying to survive as England and France competed for domination over the New World.

Chapter 6

The Confederacy Unravels

The dawn of the eighteenth century found all of the Iroquois nations sharply diminished in population. Battle casualties, disease, and religious conversion had reduced the Iroquois to half their strength in just a decade. And their troubles had only just begun.

By the late seventeenth century, England and France were in open competition for control of North America in a series of wars (King William's War, 1689–97; Queen Anne's War, 1702–13; King George's War, 1744–48; and the French and Indian War, 1754–63) that would last almost a century. The Iroquois, ever-mindful that they were the "true" residents of the Americas, were confounded by the European powers' quest for supremacy. "You think that the Axe-Makers [Europeans] are the eldest in the country and the greatest in possession," said an Iroquois leader to the governor of Canada. "We Human Beings are the first, and we are the eldest and the greatest. These parts and countries were inhabited and trod

upon by the Human Beings before there were any Axe-Makers."[51]

As England and France fought for control over the Americas, the Iroquois became what historian Douglas Edward Leach calls "unwitting victims of European power politics."[52] Village leaders became increasingly powerless to hold communities together or to uphold the promises of the Covenant Chain. The American Revolution pitted Iroquois nations against one another, shattering the peace agreement under which the Iroquois had lived for centuries. This was the final straw. The League of Five Nations would not survive.

Iroquois Diplomacy

Even as the Europeans waged war, the Iroquois maintained their position of dominance among the Native American tribes in the northeastern United States. Their strength lay in their ability to play one European power off another. "The Six Nations, or League of the Iroquois are

In the late seventeenth century, England and France fought for control of North America in a series of wars, including the French and Indian War (pictured).

frequently cited as masters of the play-off policy," concludes scholar H. A. Vernon. "For most of the eighteenth century . . . the Iroquois maintained their power and independence, which kept the colonies nearest to them watchful and respectful."[53]

Central to Iroquois diplomacy, according to historian Dean R. Snow, was the premise that

> no treaty settled anything once and for all. The Iroquois regarded friendship as a condition that needed constant nurturing and renewal, not to

mention a steady flow of essential goods. In the absence of new treaties the Iroquois believed that things would soon devolve into their natural state of war.[54]

This "natural state of war" seemed to permeate eighteenth-century America.

There is evidence that, just as the Iroquois played off European interests against one another, so too the Europeans in the Americas took advantage of the animosities among the Native American tribes. After King George's War left the

Iroquois badly beaten, one Frenchman observed, "Those who allege that the destruction of the Iroquois would promote the interest of the Colonies of New France are strangers to the true interest of that Country; for if that were once accomplish'd, the Savages who are now the French Allies would turn their greatest Enemies."[55] In other words, as long as other Indians feared the Iroquois, they would ally themselves with the French against them.

A Policy of Neutrality

When fighting broke out between France and England over territorial claims at the end of the seventeenth century, both nations looked to their Indian allies to join them in battle. To the Iroquois, however, neither the French nor the English seemed a promising ally. As historian Douglas Edward Leach explains:

Basically, the Iroquois were impressed with French strength in the West and alarmed by the mounting English appetite for more wilderness land. They now realized that if either the French or the English should become supreme in America, their own future would be seriously threatened. Sensing that they themselves might constitute a balance of power in the imperial rivalry, the Iroquois began feeling their way toward a position of neutrality that would permit them to continue their profitable economic relationship with the English and yet stand clear of war's destruction.[56]

The Iroquois chiefs voted to remain neutral, a policy they would maintain for well over half a century. They continued to trade with whichever side offered them the greatest value for their furs. In 1701 they signed a treaty with the French, which allowed them to travel freely to Montreal to engage in trade, but they also continued to keep up relations with the British.

In an attempt to consolidate their power, the Iroquois extended the Covenant Chain westward to the peoples in the Ohio Valley and the Upper Great Lakes. The new peace gave the Iroquois access to the hunting grounds in the Ohio Valley. The Iroquois allowed the Indians who lived to their west to pass through their territory on their way to European trading centers, but demanded furs in exchange for the food and shelter they provided. Having made peace with the tribes to their west, the Iroquois turned attention to their south, working with colonial governments to bring the Indians who lived there under their authority through the Covenant Chain.

But the official policy of neutrality was under constant strain, as individual bands of villagers joined the fight. The Mohawk living in Canada had already become strong allies of New France. France tended to treat the Indians better than England did, and thus was able to win over several other Iroquois villages as well as the Algonquian and other northeastern Indians. The Mohawk who remained in New York, however, were staunch allies of England—in later years, the English often referred to them as "the faithful Mohawks."

Four Indian Kings Lately Arriv'd

European attitudes toward the American Indians were highly inconsistent. The Native American people were often described as uncivilized savages, yet they were treated as royalty when this was deemed in the best interest of European nations. The following description of the visit of four Native Americans to Europe is reprinted from National Geographic's *The World of the American Indian.*

"London's Daily Courant in 1710 capitalized news that set the city agog. A century earlier William Shakespeare had noted Europe's curiosity about Indians; his jester in The Tempest jibed at people who 'when they will not give a doit [an English coin] to relieve a lame beggar . . . will lay out ten to see a dead Indian.' Now here were four live ones, lauded as rulers of their realms, come for a diplomatically vital audience with Queen Anne.

The delegation 'made a great bruit [noise] thro' the whole kingdom.' Hawkers peddled handbills extolling their 'exquisite Sense, and a quick Apprehension.' Ballads were written about them. They attended opera, heard concerts, enjoyed marionettes, visited hospitals, had portraits 'Done from ye Life' by Dutch artist John Verelst on commission from the queen.

Three were Mohawks, one a Mahican. Various spellings mark their Indian names. But they also were known by English ones: John of Canajoharie, whom Verelst painted with bow in hand and wolf totem in the background. Hendrick, also a wolf and the ranking sachem of the group in ability and influence, depicted in black court dress. Nicholas, a Mahican of the turtle clan. Brant, a bear, whose elaborate tattoos won 'not . . . so much Terror as Regard.'

The visit was a ploy by colonial leaders to generate crown enthusiasm for the border struggle against the French and to impress the chiefs with English might. Both aims succeeded. Redcoats did conquer Canada. And a long alliance saw Brant's grandson Joseph lead Iroquois warriors on Britain's side in the Revolution.

The four kings went home loaded with gifts that ranged from scarlet cloaks to a 'Magick Lanthorn with Pictures.' In turn they presented to the queen 'Necklaces . . . and other Curiosities,' including belts of wampum. The latter served to seal their words, as was the Indian custom."

The increasing pressure also weakened the links of the Covenant Chain. "The Iroquois could not control their own hunters, much less the western nations," writes Snow, "and the network of the Covenant Chain became frayed as links broke more rapidly than new ones could be forged."[57]

The Tuscaroras Join the Confederacy

If the Iroquois were unsuccessful in forging lasting bonds with their neighbors, they had better success with the Tuscarora, an Iroquoian tribe living in present-day North Carolina. By the turn of the eighteenth century, European settlers had made their life intolerable, squatting on their lands and kidnapping Tuscarora to be sold into slavery. In 1710 a group of Swiss settlers claimed a plot of land on which a Tuscarora village was already situated and evicted the villagers, renaming the town New Bern. The simmering anger of the Tuscarora exploded. In September 1711, they raided New Bern, killing more than two hundred settlers, many of whom were women and children.

The ensuing "Tuscarora Wars" were essentially a series of raids on Tuscarora villages carried out by North Carolinians, South Carolinians, and their Indian allies (mostly Yemassee). They decimated villages, seized the villagers, and sold captives into slavery. After hundreds of Tuscarora warriors were killed and hundreds more captured and sold as slaves, the majority of the remaining Tuscarora moved north to take refuge among their distant relatives in New York. The Tuscarora were formally adopted into the league of the Iroquois as a sixth nation in 1722, temporarily bolstering the population and power of the confederation.

The French and Indian War

The series of wars between England and France took their toll on all of the Indians who lived in the Northeast. Most fought alongside their European allies, often engaging in more dangerous missions than their counterparts.

Due to their superior numbers, England won the wars, but the terms of the treaties often were ambiguous, and peace between the wars was fleeting. Just six years after the King George's War ended—in 1754—war was rekindled in what the English called the French and Indian War. After seven years of fighting, England emerged as the decisive victor, and France ceded all disputed land claims. With France no longer part of the equation, the Iroquois' strategy of playing off the French and English against one another came to an end.

Those who had sided with France feared English retaliation and prepared for the worst. Pontiac, an Ottawa war chief, led a group of Indians, including a large contingent of Seneca, in an uprising. Pontiac's Indians raided English settlements and captured several English forts in the west. An estimated two thousand civilians and more than four hundred soldiers were killed before England quelled the uprisings. (It is not known how many Indians lost their lives.) As a punishment, England forced some of the Indians, including the Seneca, to cede territory to the Crown.

To avoid further disturbances, the king issued a statement known as the Proclamation of 1763, according to which the land west of the Appalachian Mountains would be "reserved" for the Indians "as their Hunting Grounds."[58] Although the Indians

Ottawa war chief Pontiac (right, center) led uprisings against the English during which he raided English settlements and captured English forts.

may have been appeased temporarily, the promise proved to be hollow. No sooner were the terms of the Proclamation of 1763 made public than land speculators and settlers poured across the mountains to stake their claim to the land. With no troops on hand (and perhaps no will), the English government was powerless to enforce the new policy. The English policy simply aggravated tension that was brewing among its American colonists.

A Revolution Breaks Out

Throughout the colonies, settlers were becoming increasingly angry about the way England governed its North American sub-

jects. In an effort to pay for the costly wars waged over the last century, England began to levy new taxes on the American colonists. These measures were very unpopular with the colonists, whose ire increased to the point of open rebellion. In April 1775, an armed confrontation between English troops and American colonists in Lexington, Massachusetts, touched off the American Revolution. Both sides courted Indian allies during the ensuing war.

Once again, the Iroquois attempted at first to maintain a neutral stance. As Little Abraham, a Mohawk leader, explained, it was "the determination of the Six Nations, not to take any part, but as it is a family affair, to sit still and see you fight it out."⁵⁹ The Iroquois referred to the war as a "dispute between two brothers"—a "quarrel" that seemed "unnatural."⁶⁰

Once again, however, their neutrality was tested. The Seneca leader Sagoyewatha described the Iroquois quandary to the American colonists:

> [T]he war has come to our doors. . . . If we sit still on our lands, and take no means of redress, the British, following the customs of you white people, will hold them by conquest; and you, if you conquer Canada, will hold them on the same principles, as conquered from the British.⁶¹

Sagoyewatha's words would prove prophetic.

Indian Involvement in the Revolutionary War

The six Iroquois nations could not agree on a course of action. The Oneida and Tuscarora sided with the Americans, but the Mohawk, Cayuga, Onondaga, and Seneca decided at council in June 1775 to join the English cause. They appointed as war chief Joseph Brant, a Mohawk leader with strong ties to England. In contrast to previous wars, the Iroquois would find themselves fighting one another in hand-to-hand combat.

The April 1775 confrontation in Lexington, Massachusetts, between English troops and American colonists began the American Revolution.

☀ Joseph Brant

Born in 1742 to a Mohawk Wolf clan chief, Joseph Brant, whose Mohawk name was Thayendanegea ("Two Sticks of Wood Bound Together") became an integral part of Iroquois history. It was largely through Brant's influence that four of the six nations of the confederacy sided with England. It was also Brant who, after the American Revolution, led a large contingent of Mohawk and others to Canada to establish a village at what is now the Six Nations Reserve near Montreal. And it was Brant who encouraged the people to adjust to a new way of life there, leasing land to whites and farming the land.

Brant's position as a leader can be attributed in part to his ability to fit in both Indian and white circles. He was raised in a traditional longhouse at Canajoharie near the Ohio River, where he learned hunting, fishing, trapping, canoeing, and all the other skills of an Iroquois hunter and warrior. Yet, white settlers had for some time settled in nearby areas, so he grew accustomed also to their ways. In fact, his grandfather had been among a small contingent of Indians who visited Queen Anne's court in England.

When his sister, Molly, married Sir William Johnson, the British superintendent of northern Indian affairs, Brant, who was only twelve, went to live with them. In 1761 he set off for Wheelock's Indian Charity School in Lebanon, Connecticut (the precursor to Dartmouth College). There, he learned to read and write both English and the Mohawk language and converted to Christianity. He would continue his quest to translate the Bible into Mohawk late into his life.

In 1774, Sir William Johnson died, and the nephew appointed as his replacement chose Joseph Brant as his aide. Shortly afterward, Brant accompanied Guy Johnson to England, where, like his grandfather, he was received as an important national leader and treated as a celebrity.

Because he believed that England might defend the Iroquois' hold on its land, Brant was a staunch supporter of England during the Revolutionary War. When he returned home from England in 1776, he traveled from one Iroquois village to another to encourage them to take up England's cause. Brant was commissioned a British colonel and led forces in raids on the materials and supplies of American troops.

Following the Revolutionary War, Brant led a contingent of pro-English Iroquois to Canada, where he established a settlement near Montreal. He became a leader of this new settlement, encouraging men to adapt to the ways of the whites in order to survive.

The four nations that sided with England were valuable allies during battle. But they also proved almost impossible to control. "Although they promised . . . that they would refrain from unnecessary cruelty," writes a historian about one battle scene, "the Senecas and some of the Mohawks ran amok, scalping, dismembering, even indulging in ritual cannibalism."[62] A Hessian officer observed, "It did not make any difference to the Indians, if they attacked a subject loyal to the king, or one friendly to the rebels; they set fire to all their homes, took away everything, killed the cattle."[63]

Not surprisingly, American forces retaliated against such destructive massacres, raiding Iroquois villages and venting their anger on the civilian inhabitants. "They put to death all the women and children," lamented an Onondaga chief after a 1778 raid, "excepting some of the young women, whom they carried away for the use of their soldiers and were afterwards put to death in a more shameful manner."[64] In 1779, commander of the American forces George Washington ordered the American troops to invade Iroquois territory and to destroy their villages.

The English were unable to defend the Iroquois. "Once the British had gotten the Indians into the war," historian Barbara Graymont concludes, "the sad fact was that they had not the forces readily available to assist them in [the event of] any large-scale invasion of their [Iroquois] territory."[65] American troops drove the Iroquois west, where they lived out the winter in squalid refugee camps sponsored by the English. They also succeeded in increasing the Iroquois' desire for revenge. The following spring, Joseph Brant led raids on Oneida and Tuscarora villages to punish them for their role as American allies. The Law of Great Peace lay in tatters.

A Broken Confederacy

In 1783 the Treaty of Paris ended the Revolutionary War. England conceded to the United States all the land between the Allegheny Mountains and the Mississippi River. The treaty made no provisions at all for the Iroquois, an omission that the pro-English Iroquois saw as a betrayal. Joseph Brant said that the retreat of the English left them "between two Hells."[66] He summarized their disappointment: "Every man of us thought that, by fighting for the King, we should ensure for ourselves and children a good inheritance."[67]

This relief from the pedestal of a statue of Benjamin Franklin depicts Franklin signing the Treaty of Paris. The treaty made no provisions for the Iroquois.

The departure of England left the Iroquois confederacy in ruins. The victorious Americans claimed that the Treaty of Paris rendered void any previous agreements made between the Iroquois and England or colonial governments and entitled them to Iroquois lands. Even those who had sided with the Americans would find themselves with little bargaining power as they struggled to hold onto their ancestral homeland.

Worse was the loss of power. The Covenant Chain could not be mended, and a new confederation in the Ohio Valley took over as the voice of the Indians. The League of Five Nations—a union that had served the Iroquois well for more than three hundred years—had ceased to exist in 1777, when the chiefs "covered their fire" at Onondaga.

After the war, Joseph Brant led a large group of Mohawk and other Iroquois to Canada, where they settled on a small stretch of land at Grand River, Ontario, which had been set aside for their use by the English government. (Today, this is known as the Six Nations Reserve). There, the Iroquois rekindled the fire representing the confederacy. Another fire was ignited at Buffalo Creek in western New York. The Iroquois confederacy had permanently and decisively broken apart.

Chapter 7

Decline and Renewal

The lands on which the Iroquois lived were now in the hands of Americans. Already, this land was but a small portion of what the Iroquois had once occupied. "Our hearts grieve us when we consider what small parcel of lands is remaining to us,"[68] complained one Mohawk leader as early as 1730. The gradual encroachment on Iroquois territory would continue unabated over the next century. Historian Francis Jennings lauds the relative success of the Iroquois fighting against such imposing forces: "That the Iroquois were able, for another half century, to cope with the inexorable pressures of speculators, homesteaders, and squatters is testimony to their remarkable political and diplomatic skills."[69] But the Iroquois needed far more than diplomacy to resist the land-hungry Americans.

As they dealt with land speculators, the Indians tried to strike the best deals they could, but many of the people with whom they negotiated were unfair at best. Some were plainly unscrupulous, plying the In-dians with alcohol until they were ready to sign over land for far less than it was worth. Others manipulated the phrasing of the deeds to strip land from the Indians without their consent or knowledge. Contrary to what many people today believe, the Iroquois were aware of their loss. "We know our lands are now become more valuable," said the Onondaga leader Canasatego. "The white people think we do not know their value; but we are sensible that the land is everlasting, and the few goods we receive for it are soon worn out and gone."[70]

The Europeans and Americans who swindled the Indians out of their land rationalized their actions. Some claimed that the Indians were nomads with no tradition of land ownership. Others argued that the Native Americans were not making the best use of the land—that European methods of farming were far more effective. Others even claimed that white ownership of the land was God's will, pointing to the spread of disease as proof. "Thus was God pleased to smite our enemies," said one English colonist, "and to give us their land for an Inheritance."[71] Centuries of custom and tradition were insufficient in the face of such reasoning. By the turn of the nineteenth century, the Indians lacked the political, military, or economic means to overcome the steady advance of the settlers, backed as it was by the might of the U.S. government.

Postwar Treaties

A year after the American Revolution, representatives of the new U.S. government arranged to meet with the four nations that had sided with England—the Mohawk, Cayuga, Onondaga, and Seneca—at Fort Stanwix. Here, they explained that the Iroquois' previous treaties had been suspended and the claims on the land defended by such treaties were no longer valid. With no choice but to agree to the terms the United States put forth at the Treaty of Fort Stanwix, the Iroquois ceded much of their land in western New York and Pennsylvania and all of their land in Ohio.

When they learned of the Treaty of Fort Stanwix, the Six Nations council that had assumed leadership for the Iroquois tribes

At Fort Stanwix, a reconstruction of which is shown here, representatives of the U.S. government met with the four Iroquois nations that had sided with England.

On Education

From the beginning, many schools and universities in the colonies included the education of Native Americans as part of their charter. At a 1744 meeting in Lancaster, Pennsylvania, the Onondaga sachem Canasatego explained to the commissioners from Virginia why the Iroquois had decided to turn down their offer to educate some of their young men at the college in Williamsburg. This excerpt is taken from Robert W. Venables' essay "American Indian Influences on the America of the Founding Fathers," in *Exiled in the Land of the Free*.

"Our ideas of this kind of education happen not to be the same with yours. We have had some experience of it: Several of our young people were formerly brought up at the colleges of the northern provinces; they were instructed in all your sciences; but when they came back to us, they were bad runners, ignorant of every means of living in the woods, unable to bear either cold or hunger, knew neither how to build a cabin, take a deer, nor kill an enemy, spoke our language imperfectly; were therefore neither fit for hunters, warriors, or counsellors; they were totally good for nothing. We are however not the less obliged by your king's offer, though we decline accepting it; and to show our grateful sense of it, if the gentlemen of Virginia will send us a dozen of their sons, we will take great care of their education, instruct them in all we know, and make men of them."

still in the United States was greatly angered. The council chiefs argued that the 1794 treaty was invalid because the Six Nations had not given it their consent. But the U.S. government ignored their protests, just as it would ignore similar protests of other Indian nations in the many decades to come.

The Treaty of Fort Stanwix was just the beginning of a gradual erosion of the Iroquois lands in New York. In agreements with private land companies and New York State officials, the Iroquois reluctantly, but voluntarily, sold most of their remaining land, keeping only small tracts for themselves. In addition, the Iroquois still left in Ohio pulled up roots and moved to Indian Territory (now Oklahoma).

This emigration was not voluntary. Rather, it was undertaken because of pressure resulting from a new U.S. policy that called for the forced relocation of nearly one hundred thousand Native Americans from New York and ten other states and territories. The so-called removal policy, enacted as the Indian Removal Act of 1830, was supposed to ensure peace between the United States and the Indian tribes (since Indian villages would be far from American settlements). It also offered U.S. citizens the chance to acquire at prices far below market value the rich lands that would be vacated by the Indians. The years following 1830 saw many blatant attempts to cheat Indians on sales of the lands from which they were being removed.

A Swindle at Buffalo Creek

In 1838 the Ogden Land Company negotiated a treaty at Buffalo Creek that deprived the Seneca of all their remaining reservations and offered them land in Kansas in return. The treaty was clearly fraudulent, for some of the chiefs' signatures were later shown to be forgeries. Moreover, real signatures had been obtained under duress: The U.S. government representative had threatened that the president of the United States "will punish you as a father punishes his disobedient child, unless you do as he desires; he will turn your face where he wishes you to go, before he stops punishing you."[72] He also told the Indians that authority over the Iroquois would be turned over to New York State, resulting in the loss of federal benefits and protection of their land. Even in the face of such threats, fewer than half of the Seneca chiefs had signed the treaty.

The Seneca were outraged. With the help of Quaker missionaries living among them, they fought to nullify the treaty. In 1842 a compromise was struck: the Ogden Land Company returned to the Seneca their lands at Allegany and Cattaraugus but kept the land at Buffalo Creek and Tonawanda. Several years later, the Seneca repurchased these lands from the Ogden Land Company.

The Buffalo Creek incident would change forever the political structure of the Seneca at Allegany and Cattaraugus. Fearing that the traditional chiefs would again sell their land from under them, the Seneca moved to an elected system of government, ruled by a council of sixteen elected chiefs. The Tonawanda Seneca adopted a modified form of government with some elected chiefs and some traditional chiefs. Other Iroquois groups have also changed their form of government to an elected system, but the Onondaga and Tuscarora have continued with the tradition of having clan mothers nominate the chiefs. Debate over the governing system continues among many Iroquois today; in fact, both forms of government exist on the Six Nations Reserve, where the hereditary council is primarily a ceremonial body.

The Six Nations Reserve

At the Six Nations Reserve in Grand River, Ontario, each nation set up its own village, and the Iroquois attempted to reestablish their culture and system of government. But their goal to live as they once had was unattainable.

Although the 675,000 acres at Grand River was larger than the U.S. reservations, it was still much smaller than what the Mohawk and others had left behind. There was too little game to support hunting, and most of the men refused to take up the "women's work" of farming.

Joseph Brant, who emerged as a leader of the Six Nations Reserve, believed that the men would have to forgo their traditional attitudes and acquire new skills if the Iroquois were to survive. He proposed selling and leasing tracts of the Grand River lands to non-Indian farmers. Not only would this bring in much-needed money, but it also would help acquaint the Iroquois with the farming techniques they would need in the future.

On some levels, Brant's plan was a success. The reservation earned money. Iroquois men began farming, and agricultural output gradually increased. In fact, by the middle of the nineteenth century, the Grand River Reserve was selling surpluses in nearby urban areas.

But the plan also had one regrettable long-term consequence: More than 350,000 acres of reservation land passed into the possession of non-Indians.

Eating Away at Tradition

Isolated on their reservations, the Iroquois harked back to the days before the white man had set foot on the turtle's back. Canasatego, an Onondaga elder, lamented that the Iroquois had "lived before [the Europeans] came among us, and as well, or better. We had then room enough, and plenty of deer, which was easily caught; and tho' we had not knives, hatchets, or guns, such as we have now, yet we had knives of stone, and bows and arrows, and those served our uses as well then as the English ones do now."[73]

But it was too late to turn back. All of the means by which the Iroquois had survived for centuries had disappeared. They could not practice their traditional agriculture because they could not move their villages when the fields were exhausted. As colonists settled the lands around them, they no longer had access to forests in which to hunt or streams in which fish flowed freely. "The new landscape wrecked Iroquois morale," writes Snow. "Without either corporate or individual independence, and without their traditional means to gain power and prestige, many succumbed to alcoholism. There

As the Iroquois moved to reservations, they struggled to keep their traditional ways of life intact. Here, a Seneca chief is shown in traditional dress.

☼ The Civil War

Native Americans have continued to engage in combat during the wars waged by the United States. This excerpt from Dean R. Snow's *The Iroquois* reveals the effect of participation in the Civil War on Iroquois men.

"The Iroquois had participated in Euro-American conflicts since early in the seventeenth century. Prior to the War of 1812 their roles had been largely those of scouts and guerillas. By the time of the American Civil War, they were serving in ordinary cavalry and infantry units, fully integrated with Euro-Americans and receiving the same pay. . . .

Army service provided the outlet that combat had always given the Iroquois. It was time away from claustrophobic reservation life and the tensions of ever-present factional disputes. It was also a source of cash for young men having little other access to it.

The Iroquois were at first not allowed to join the army because no law could be found permitting it. . . . At the time, Indians were not considered citizens, and could not successfully apply for citizenship. In 1862 the government finally decided to allow Indians to enlist, although they were not covered by the draft. Various Iroquois fought in nearly every battle after March 1862. . . .

The Civil War moved the Iroquois who stayed home away from subsistence farming and towards market-oriented production, just as it did other farmers. The aftermath brought a new wave of non-Indian population increase, and with it new pressures on Indian land. The war had done nothing to halt the decline in their fortunes, but it set a pattern of voluntary service by Iroquois in the United States military that persists today."

they languished, without faith in their traditional national leaders, and without a single coherent League of Nations."[74]

Iroquois men were particularly hard hit by the changes brought about by reservation life. While women could continue with their traditional responsibilities of tending to the children and the fields, the traditional roles of men were stripped from them. There was no hunting, no warring with other Indian nations, no need for diplomacy. Reservation

life annihilated the traditional lifestyle of the once-powerful Iroquois and struck at the self-respect of its once-proud men.

Handsome Lake Brings the "Good Message"

As the old way of life deteriorated, Ganiodaiyo, or Handsome Lake, a Seneca medicine man, was one of the many Indians who succumbed to alcoholism. In the spring of 1799, Handsome Lake collapsed and appeared dead. When he awoke from his coma, he recounted a vision in which the Creator had spoken to him. The Creator told him to give up alcohol and spread the news about how the Iroquois were to live. Because the Iroquois placed much stock in dreams, they listened attentively to what Handsome Lake had to say. Within a few months, he had several more visions—visions that would save the Iroquois from ruin.

Handsome Lake told of a new code: the "Gai'wiio" or "Good Message." He repeated the Creator's instruction for men to participate in agriculture and to domesticate animals. He embraced the benefits of European-style education and agricultural practices; emphasized family unity and loyalty, with marriage (not a matrilineal hierarchy) at the core; and preached abstinence from alcohol. In addition, Handsome Lake said that sacred ceremonial rites should be continued. The consequences of abandoning traditional Iroquois ceremonies would be the destruction of the world by fire.

Over the next fifteen years, Handsome Lake worked as an Iroquois prophet, bringing the word of the Gai'wiio to the reservations. Known as the New Religion among the Iroquois, Handsome Lake's teachings brought renewed sense of self to

White men often included liquor in their trades with Native Americans, or encouraged them to get drunk in order to secure better terms in their deals.

the Iroquois. As James Wilson summarizes, "His message allowed [the Iroquois] to adapt, in some measure, to the new society which was rapidly establishing itself around them, and at the same time, to maintain their own identity."[75] The New Religion would take several decades to spread to Iroquois reservations, but the spiritual renewal that resulted enabled the Iroquois to adapt, persevere, and, in time, regain a sense of pride in their cultural heritage.

"Civilizing the Savage"

By the end of the nineteenth century, the U.S. government had again changed its policy toward Native Americans. Whereas it had once sought to resolve the "Indian problem" by moving all Native Americans west of the Mississippi River, now it sought to rid Indians of their "Indianness" by "civilizing" them and assimilating them into white America. Policy makers believed that the way to achieve this was to encourage Indians to speak English and to worship a Christian god.

Reformers had worked for many years helping the Iroquois adapt by teaching them new skills. In the early 1800s, Quaker volunteers joined Seneca villages along the New York–Pennsylvania border. The volunteers worked among the Seneca, teaching them how to read and write. The Quakers also promoted the idea of men working in agriculture and stressed the importance of morality, sobriety, and family. Similarly, the New York Mission Society situated ministers and teachers to the Tuscarora Reservation and the Buffalo Creek Reservation to teach agricultural and domestic skills. On the Grand River Reserve, Protestant missionaries built their first churches in 1827 and set up a school in 1831.

But now reform was linked with stripping the Indians of their culture completely. Indian schools were designed to teach children how to behave like whites. "The Indian high school rightly conducted will be a gateway out from the desolation of the reservation into assimilation with our national life,"[76] explained a nineteenth-century commissioner of Indian Affairs. The most effective way to accomplish this was through boarding schools. Here, students were given new "American" names and forbidden to speak their own languages. Boys had their hair cut, and both boys and girls were forced to wear "American" clothing. Strict discipline was used to curb "savage" ways.

Like other Indian tribes, the Iroquois resented the Indian schools. Minnie Kellogg, an Iroquois who was sent to white schools, called them "spirit-breaking." She went on to denounce the Indian Service, "whose one aim was to 'civilize' the race youth, by denouncing his parents, his customs, his people wholesale, and filling the vacuum they had created with their vulgar notions of what constituted civilization."[77]

As time passed, however, an increasing number of Indian children would be educated in the ways of the whites. Even traditionalists would come to wonder if the old ways were null and void in the new world into which they had been thrown.

Indians Must Be Indians

Mary Jemison, the daughter of Irish immigrants who was adopted by the Seneca in 1758, described the debilitating effect of alcohol and the sometimes well-meaning attempts to "civilize" the Indians. The following excerpt from her story, as told to James E. Seaver, is from *Native Americans*, edited by William Dudley.

"[W]e lived without any of those jealousies, quarrels, and revengeful battles between families and individuals which have been common in the Indian tribes since the introduction of ardent spirits [alcohol] among them.

The use of ardent spirits amongst the Indians, and the attempts which have been made to civilize and christianize them by the white people, has constantly made them worse and worse; increased their vices, and robbed them of many of their virtues; and will ultimately produce their extermination. I have seen, in a number of instances, the effects of education upon some of our Indians, who were taken when young, from their families, and placed at school before they had had an opportunity to contract many Indian habits, and kept there till they arrived to manhood; but I have never seen one of those but what was an Indian in every respect after he returned. Indians must and will be Indians, in spite of all the means that can be used for their cultivation in the sciences and arts."

The Allotment of Property

Moving land from tribal ownership to individual ownership was considered another means for civilizing the Indians. One reformer explained:

There is an immense moral training that comes from the use of property. . . . [T]he Indian must learn that he has no right to give until he has earned, and that he has no right to eat until he has worked for his bread. . . . We have found it necessary, as one of the first steps in developing a stronger personality in the Indian, *to make him responsible for property. . . .* This is the first great step in the education of the race.[78]

Both Canada and the United States soon had mechanisms in place to give families ownership of the land. In Canada, each male head of household living on reserve land was given 100 acres. In the United States, the General Allotment Act of 1887, or Dawes Act, stipulated that each household head should be allotted 160 acres.

Described by Theodore Roosevelt as a "mighty pulverising engine to break up the tribal mass,"[79] the Dawes Act officially

Ely Parker

Ely Samuel Parker, also known as Ha-sa-no-an-da, was a Seneca tribal and military leader who became known for his work furthering the causes of both the United States and the American Indian. Parker served the Union during the Civil War and wrote the final copy of the surrender terms of the Confederate army. Parker later reported that Robert E. Lee was surprised to see a Native American in such a prominent position at the surrender. In 1869, Parker was appointed U.S. commissioner of Indian affairs, becoming the first Native American to hold this post.

Parker studied to become a lawyer, but he was denied admittance to the bar because he was not a U.S. citizen. (U.S. citizenship was a prerequisite for the practice of law, but Native Americans were not automatically granted citizenship until 1924.) Shut off from a career in law, Parker instead became a successful civil engineer and worked on a number of prominent projects including the Erie Canal.

When the Civil War broke out, Parker wanted to join the Union forces, but he was at first unable to do so because of his race. He had previously met Ulysses S. Grant, however, and was able to use his connections to gain a commission as captain in 1863 under General Grant's command. He began his service as an engineer, but was soon assigned to work as Grant's military aide. It is in this capacity that he drafted the terms of the confederacy's surrender. When Grant was elected president, he appointed Parker as commissioner of Indian affairs. During his two years in this post, the Seneca leader worked diligently to establish better relations between the government and Indian agencies. In reforming the corrupt agency, Parker made many enemies, however, and he resigned under pressure in 1871.

Perhaps Parker's legacy of leadership is not surprising given his ancestry. A direct descendant of Handsome Lake, Parker was also related to the tribal leader Cornplanter and the great orator Red Jacket. He grew up on the Tonawanda Reservation, where he was taught English at a missionary school and was taught to hunt and fish by his older relatives. He also learned about the Seneca people and his famous ancestors.

Parker shared his knowledge of his people's native ways with Lewis Henry Morgan, a young lawyer interested in American Indian culture. The result was a widely respected account of the Iroquois entitled *League of the Ho-de-no-saunee*. Published in 1851, the book is considered to be one of the first anthropological studies of any American Indian group, and its author is called the father of American anthropology.

was meant to encourage the primacy of nuclear families and the transition to family farms, but it had another, darker intent. "The main purpose of [the Dawes Act]," reported the minority members of the House Committee on Indian Affairs, "is not to help the Indian, . . . so much as it is to provide a method for getting at the valuable Indian lands and opening them up to white settlement."[80] By allowing the sale of leftover land to non-Indians after allotment, the legislation in effect stole additional lands from Indians, particularly those living on large reservations in the western United States.

Once the land was under private ownership, the Indians had to pay local taxes on it. Many could not afford to pay and were forced to sell the land. In this way, the Oneida living in Wisconsin lost 95 percent of their lands; by 1934, they had a mere ninety acres. Because previous treaties had given the Ogden Land Company the exclusive right to buy Iroquois land in New York, the Iroquois in that state were spared the worst of the Dawes Act.

The reforms put in place during the nineteenth century—those that were well intentioned and those that were not—signaled a further assault on Iroquois culture and native pride. Stressing individual rather than communal ownership of the land and allotting the land only to nuclear families resulted in an erosion of tribal unity and the extended family. Furthermore, the legislation undermined the traditional family structure in which women were responsible for food production and owned the land. The struggle to adjust would continue for many years to come.

Chapter 8

Adaptation and Tradition

By the beginning of the twentieth century, the American Indian population had sunk to its lowest level ever. The Iroquois were crowded into a few small plots of land, which were inadequate to support their traditional lifestyle. Policies to break up tribal lands, destroy Indian culture, and educate children to think and act like whites had

Native Americans pose for a picture at Carlisle School, an institution that attempted to educate its students to think and act like whites.

taken their toll on the sense of pride that once dominated the Iroquois character.

While previous centuries had been characterized by policies to annihilate Indian culture—and often the Indian himself—the twentieth century brought renewed attention to the plight of Indians. The Dawes Act was seen as ineffectual, but reformers disagreed about what policies should replace it. The Indians were caught in the middle of an unfolding drama as reformers, often with the best of intentions, changed their minds time and again on whether to assimilate Indians or allow them to govern themselves. This debate continues today.

In the midst of this change, the Iroquois have struggled to balance tradition while adapting to modern life. "It has been pointed out that culture constantly changes," observes one Onondaga chief. "It is not the same today as it was a hundred years ago. . . . We continue to survive."[81]

Life on the Reservation

Unable to support themselves through traditional activities, the Iroquois, like other Native Americans, have struggled to make their way in the midst of a changing economic system. At the turn of the century, reservation life was characterized by a multitude of problems, including alcoholism, high unemployment, crowded schools, inadequate health care, poverty, and disease. Two yardsticks for measuring the health of a community—life expectancy and infant mortality—lagged far behind national averages.

In 1928 the U.S. secretary of the interior commissioned an independent research organization to study the plight of the Indians. The resulting report, called the Meriam Report after the director of the survey, concluded that "an overwhelming majority of the Indians are poor, even extremely poor."[82] The report blamed the Bureau of Indian Affairs for much of the problem, focusing particular attention on the destructive effect of the allotment policies under the Dawes Act. According to the report, the policies had failed to recognize "the strength of the ancient system of communal ownership,"[83] and, consequently, "resulted in much loss of land and an enormous increase in the details of administration without a compensating advance in the economic ability of the Indians."[84]

The underlying assumption of the Meriam Report was that assimilation was the best course of action. But the report went beyond the current understanding of what the process of assimilation entailed. Its authors wrote that American leaders should "recognize the good in the educational and social life of the Indians in their religion and ethics, and . . . see to develop it and build on it rather than to crush out all that is Indian. The Indians have much to contribute to the dominant civilization."[85]

A New Deal

From the start, reformers sought to remedy the misfortunes of those on the reservation. The state of New York also attempted to alleviate the Iroquois' plight with programs in health, education, transportation, and social services. In 1932 the children at Tonawanda became the first of New York's Indians to be integrated into the local public school system. Such efforts came at a high cost to the Native Americans, however. The Indians' growing dependency and declining self-sufficiency made them increasingly vulnerable to outside forces. Again and again, New York State tried to expand its jurisdiction over the reservations.

The economic depression that left many Americans without means in the 1930s would plunge American Indians further into poverty and despair. It would also serve as a wake-up call as all Americans began to look to their government for assistance. John Collier, the commissioner of Indian affairs, insisted that Indians be included in the "New Deal" that President Franklin Delano Roosevelt promised all Americans. Upon becoming commissioner of Indian affairs in 1933, Collier stated that he wanted

to use the monies appropriated by the Congress for Indians as to enable them, on good, adequate lands of their own, to earn decent livelihoods and lead self-respecting, organized

John Collier (third from left), commissioner of Indian affairs in the 1930s, wanted FDR's New Deal to include and benefit Native Americans.

The Indian Reorganization Act of 1934

The Indian Reorganization Act changed the nature of the U.S. government's relationship with Native Americans. The legislation ended the policy of allotting tribal lands to individuals and provided for tribal self-government. The following provisions of the legislation are reprinted from William Dudley's *Native Americans.*

"An act to conserve and develop Indian lands and resources; to extend to Indians the right to form business and other organizations; to establish a credit system for Indians; to grant certain rights of home rule to Indians; to provide for vocational education for Indians and for other purposes. . . .

That hereafter no land of any Indian reservations, created or set apart by treaty or agreement with the Indians . . . shall be allotted in severalty to any Indian.

SEC. 3: The Secretary of the Interior, if he shall find it to be in the public interest,

is hereby authorized to restore to tribal ownership the remaining surplus lands of any Indian reservation heretofore opened, or authorized to be opened. . . .

SEC. 16: Any Indian tribe, or tribes, residing on the same reservation shall have the right to organize for its common welfare, and may adopt an appropriate constitution and bylaws, which shall become effective when ratified by a majority vote of the adult members of the tribe, or of the Indians residing on such reservation . . . at a special election authorized and called by the Secretary of the Interior. . . .

The constitution adopted by said tribe shall also vest in such tribe or its tribal council the following rights and powers: To employ legal counsel . . .; to prevent the sale, distribution, lease, or encumbrance of tribal lands, interests in lands or other tribal assets without the consent of the tribe; and to negotiate with the Federal, State, and local Governments."

lives in harmony with their own aims and ideals, as an integral part of American life. Under such a policy, the ideal end result will be the ultimate disappearance of any need for government aid or supervision.[86]

To accomplish this goal, Collier advocated giving Indians responsibility for

their own well-being and guaranteeing them the land essential to their survival.

The Indian Reorganization Act of 1934 was the cornerstone of Collier's program. The legislation reversed the land allotment policy of the Dawes Act and provided for the organization of tribal corporations and governments. Provisions to preserve Native American heritage by reviving tribal languages and indigenous arts and crafts were included in the legislation. The bill also sought to address the high unemployment and poverty rates among Native Americans by establishing programs to put youth to work on public projects, promoting economic enterprise, providing loans for vocational training, and funding programs for Indian youth in public schools.

Unlike his predecessors, Collier put his theory to the test, asking Native American tribes to give their support through a vote. Ever protective of their independence and their sovereign status, the Iroquois of New York voted against the law. However, the funding helped the Oneida of Wisconsin obtain much-needed loans to begin businesses and improve their economic plight.

Termination

The advent of World War II thwarted the lofty goals of the Indian Reorganization Act, as funding was redirected to the war effort. But just as the war helped to spur the overall American economy, so too it helped ameliorate the plight of the Native American. In addition to the many Native Americans who went into battle, an estimated forty-six thousand found work in munitions factories or other opportunities afforded by the war effort. As a result of these opportunities, many Indians left the reservation for the first time.

But American Indians would once again face the challenge of adapting to a change in American policy. Administrators were tired of funding programs that seemingly accomplished little toward improving life on the reservation. They believed that cutting government aid would force the Indians to join mainstream society and become self-sufficient. In the 1950s, the U.S. government tried to put an end to the public assistance provided to Indians.

As part of this so-called "termination" policy, reservation Indians were offered a one-way bus ticket to urban centers and given a promise of help in finding jobs. Most Indians who took the government up on its offer found the adjustment difficult at best—poverty was the most likely outcome. More than one hundred thousand Indians relocated to cities between 1952 and 1972, but nearly a third returned to the reservation. Some moved back and forth, uncomfortable in both settings. Once again, the Iroquois avoided the worst of the results by using existing treaties to keep their status and exempt themselves from the termination policy.

Loss of Land to "Eminent Domain"

The Iroquois were less successful in putting an end to the encroachment on their lands. During the 1950s and 1960s, the Canadian, U.S., and New York State governments applied the principle of eminent domain to take additional lands from several Iroquois reservations. The concept of eminent domain asserts that government derives the right to take land for needed improvement as long as just compensation is provided to the people who are forced to cede their property.

The Mohawk tribe lost 88 acres of land to the U.S. government for construction of the St. Lawrence Seaway (pictured).

In the 1940s, the Canadian government seized land from the Mohawk reserve at Akwesasne for the construction of a bridge and customs facilities. Less than a decade later, the tribe lost another 88 acres to the U.S. government for the St. Lawrence Seaway, which was built to allow ships passage from the Great Lakes to the Atlantic Ocean. In addition to the loss of land, the Mohawk were affected by the pollution that resulted from the opening of the seaway and the growth of industries in cities along the river. The Kahnawake Reserve also lost 1,260 acres to the project, including a portion of a centuries-old village.

The Tuscarora lost over five hundred acres—a fifth of their land—when the Niagara Power Plant was built. In the 1960s, a third of the Seneca's Allegany Reservation was taken for the Kinzua Dam project, which resulted in the flooding of over nine thousand acres of their tribal homelands. About 130 families had to move away and burials had to be moved to higher ground. The growth of the interstate highway system in the 1950s also encroached on Iroquois reservations. The New York State Thruway was built through the Cattaraugus Reservation, and the Southern Tier Expressway was built through the Allegany Reservation.

The Iroquois attempted to fight the infringement on their property rights both in court and out. In 1957, the Akwesasne Mohawk bitterly protested the seizure of their lands through the public defiance of a court order. The Tuscarora also resisted the taking of this land in the courts and won an initial appeal, but in 1960 the Supreme Court overturned the ruling. Although the Tuscarora lost this battle, other Indians followed their example, fighting for their land and their rights in the courts. The Seneca won their Kinzua Dam lawsuit and were awarded over $15 million, but in their eyes this was small compensation for the loss of their traditional homeland and sacred grounds.

Lawsuits over the loss of land continue to this day. Several Indian tribes of the Northeast, including the Oneida and Cayuga, have sued states for the return of land they believe was taken from them illegally. To defend their position they cite the 1790 Indian Trade and Intercourse Act, which declared that "no sale of lands made by any Indians, or any nation or tribe of Indians within the United States, shall be valid to any person or persons, or to any state . . . held under the authority of the United States."[87] As yet, most of the Iroquois' lawsuits have been unsuccessful, but the fight continues.

Making a Living

A century ago, many Iroquois carved out a living through agriculture, and some were quite successful. Most Iroquois today have abandoned farming, however, because they cannot afford the expensive machinery needed to compete with large, modern farms. Life on the reservation continues to be hard, particularly after budgetary cutbacks reduced government services provided to Indians in the 1980s. Many Indians continue to live in poverty, and most Indian communities have a much lower standard of living than do white American communities.

On some reservations, casinos have replaced agriculture as the major economic activity. A 1987 Supreme Court ruling protects the right of Indians in states that do not forbid gambling to have gaming on their reservations. The Indian Gaming Regulatory Act of 1988 further defines the rights of the reservations. Within five years of the passage of this legislation, 124 Indian casinos had been built in twenty-four states. The Oneida Nation Casino near Green Bay was soon the largest minority-owned business in Wisconsin.

Despite the boost to the reservation economy, gambling has proved divisive in many communities—and deadly on the Mohawk reservation at Akwesasne, where the 1980s witnessed a series of violent confrontations, arson, and even a murder. James Wilson writes that gambling

> created an immense gulf between rich and poor and inflamed the centuries-old debate about what it means to be Mohawk. Anti-casino "Traditionals" accuse the opposing "Warriors" of being seduced away from their culture by American materialism, while the Warriors claim the Traditionals have been brainwashed into submission by

The Rise of Red Power

Like the Iroquois, Indians throughout North America continued to lose land to the government during the twentieth century. With this loss of land came an erosion of morale and a loss of pride.

By the 1960s and 1970s, some American Indians decided on a militant approach to resolving their centuries-old problems with the U.S. government. What became known as "red power" actually began several decades earlier, as increasing numbers of Native Americans began to mingle at boarding schools and in cities. Here, they learned that they shared common histories, common problems, and common challenges.

With this growing awareness came the emergence of several pan-Indian organizations, including the National Congress of American Indians (founded in 1944), the National Indian Youth Council (1961), and the militant American Indian Movement (founded in 1968). As skilled politicians with strong beliefs in tribal sovereignty and treaty rights, the Iroquois were involved in pan-Indian organizations from the beginning.

Tired of being treated as second-class citizens, red power advocates wanted to hold the United States to the many promises it had made over the past centuries. Their tactics varied. In 1969, seventy-eight Indians took over Alcatraz, an island off San Francisco that had once housed a federal prison, claiming it under the terms of an 1868 treaty that promised to return unused federal property to Indian control. The occupation of the site lasted two years.

During the 1960s and 1970s, many Native Americans tired of being treated unfairly and tried to hold the United States to the promises it had made them.

Although casinos have been profitable for many reservations, some Iroquois believe that the casinos are destroying traditional Native American culture.

American power: by exploiting the Euro-American addiction to gambling . . ., they argue, they are merely continuing the old struggle to protect and sustain their communities by other means.[88]

To get away from the casinos and their influence, one group of Mohawk living at Akwesasne left to establish a new community on the tribe's original homeland.

In addition to casinos, several Iroquois tribes have found stable ways to support themselves. The Mohawk, for example, are world-renowned steelworkers and have worked on bridges and skyscrapers throughout the United States and Canada. The Seneca have leased parcels of their reservation land for more than a hundred years. Among this land is the entire city of Salamanca, New York, which was under a ninety-nine year lease that expired in 1991. The Seneca have profited from their role as landlords. After releasing the property in 1992, the city of Salamanca was billed for almost $120,000 for back rent and interest.

Preserving Their Sovereignty

Throughout this turbulent history, the Iroquois have maintained their sovereignty. They remind us that they existed as independent nations long before the United States or Canada came into being and that they have never relinquished their right of self-government.

☀ High Steel Mohawk

The Iroquois have struggled to make their way among Euro-Americans. Early on, the Mohawk found an outlet in construction. In the 1880s, Mohawk living at Akwesasne found work building a new bridge in Cornwall, Ontario, and Mohawk at Kahnawake helped build the Victoria Tubular Bridge across a lower section of the St. Lawrence. The foremen at the construction sites were impressed by the Mohawk fearlessness as they climbed atop the high steel structures. An official of the Dominion Bridge Company was quoted as saying, "Putting riveting tools in the Mohawk's hands was like putting ham with eggs. They were natural-born bridgemen."

Their reputation spread quickly, and soon they were working on bridges and skyscrapers throughout the area. The wages were good, but the work was perilous. Scores of Mohawk died in the first decades of ironworking, including 33 who were killed in 1907 in the collapse of Quebec Bridge.

The Mohawk also began working on skyscrapers. They have helped build almost all of the tallest buildings in New York City: the RCA Building, Rockefeller Center, and the quarter-mile-high Empire State Building. By the middle of the century, so many Mohawk had settled in one neighborhood of Brooklyn that it became known as "Downtown Caughnawaga." Today, the Mohawk continue to work on bridges and skyscrapers across the United States and Canada.

Of course, no one really knows why the Mohawk are attracted to this line of work. Some people speculate that it captures the essence of what it is to be an Iroquois. High steel provides Mohawk with a sense of adventure, wealth, and prestige that their warrior ancestors would have appreciated.

The Mohawk have developed a reputation as talented steelworkers and have worked on many famous skyscrapers, including New York's Rockefeller Center.

As an independent nation, the Iroquois issued their own declaration of war on Germany in 1917. (Because they were not a party in the peace settlement after that war, they did not declare war at the outset of World War II.) The Iroquois also have steadfastly refused American citizenship, which was conferred in 1924 on all Indians living in the United States, and continue to view citizenship as a threat to their sovereignty. Even today, Iroquois who travel abroad carry passports issued by the Iroquois nation.

Another assault on the independent status of the Iroquois came with the passage of the Immigration Act of 1924. Designed to keep Asians out of the country, the law forbade aliens who were ineligible for citizenship to enter the United States. This included the many Indians who routinely crossed the border from Canada to visit relatives and go to their jobs. When Mohawk Paul Diabo was arrested for violating the law in 1925, he hired a lawyer to help him appeal the law. Clinton Rickard, a Tuscarora, formed the Indian Defense League of America to help Diabo. The lawyers pointed out that applying the 1924 Immigration Act to Native Americans clearly violated the Jay Treaty of 1790, which stated that the Indians living on either side of the boundary between the United States and Canada should be allowed "freely to pass and repass" into each country.

The Iroquois won their lawsuit. In 1928, Congress passed legislation to provide for the uninterrupted passage of Indians over the border. To the Iroquois, this represented recognition of their sovereignty as a nation and their rights as a people. The Iroquois celebrate and remember their hard-fought victory in a Border Crossing Ceremony each July.

Preserving Their Heritage

The Iroquois have been in contact with people of European descent for over four hundred years. From the beginning, the Iroquois married white settlers and adopted white children as members of their tribes. Today, many Iroquois blend in with their white neighbors as they commute from their reservations to jobs in nearby cities or towns. Most Iroquois children speak only English. The reservations from which they travel to school or jobs are often indistinguishable from the suburbs that surround them.

Yet, the desire to preserve their heritage continues to grow. For a long time, the Iroquois have called for the return of their wampum belts and false face masks and have built museums in which to house these and other artifacts of their culture. They also have fought to preserve their ceremonies and languages, which one Iroquois spokesman calls "the soul of the Iroquois nation. . . .Without it," he explains, "we do not have a nation, because there is knowledge . . . that does not translate into English." [89]

Despite centuries of attacks on their sovereignty, the Iroquois survive. As Dean R. Snow puts it:

The longhouse survives as an institution, just as clans survive, having persisted through expulsions, epidemics,

The Words of an Onondaga Chief

In the midst of the pressures of the late twentieth century, Iroquois leaders have held fast to their culture and worked hard to preserve their heritage. The following excerpt from a 1986 speech by Oren Lyons, an Onondaga traditional chief, illustrates the Iroquois' attempts to survive the onslaught of white settlement. This excerpt is taken from James Wilson's *The Earth Shall Weep*.

"We will determine what our culture is. It has been pointed out that culture constantly changes. It is not the same today as it was a hundred years ago. We are still a vital, active Indian society. We are not going to be put in a museum or accept your interpretation of our culture. . . .

We continue to survive. Our chief council is composed of respectable and dignified men. They are profoundly endowed with the spirit of nationhood, freedom and self-determination. When we travel about and meet with the elders from the other different nations and peoples, we find our friends.

I cannot speak for anybody but the Six Nations of Iroquois, but I can tell you that we have children who believe that they are Onondagas. We have longhouses that are full of our young people. We have a lacrosse team called the Iroquois Nationals that competes with Canada, the United States, England and Australia.

It is a fact that a small group of people in the northeast have survived an onslaught for some 490 years. They continue their original manner of government. They also drive cars, have televisions, and ride on planes. We make the bridges that you cross over and build the buildings that you live in.

So what are we? Are we traditionalists or are we assimilated? If you can get away from your categories and definitions, you will perceive us as a living and continuing society. We believe that the wampum and the ceremonial masks should be at home. We will continue our ceremonies. We have the right to exist and that right does not come from you or your government."

wars, adoptions, and hostile outside government policies. Their belts, their languages, their games, their cuisine, their dress, their character, their humor, and their fundamental sense of community all survive as well.[90]

As a new century unfolds, the Iroquois continue their centuries-old struggle to adapt to change without losing their pride, their power, or their beliefs. In their ongoing defense of their sovereignty they find the strength to carry on tradition. "We have the right to exist," Onondaga traditional chief Oren Lyons told a conference in 1986, "and that right does not come from you or [the] government."[91]

Notes

Introduction: Who Are the Iroquois?

1. Ruth M. Underhill, *Red Man's America.* Chicago: University of Chicago Press, 1971, p. 83.

Chapter 1: The Iroquois: Past and Present

2. Quoted in Dean R. Snow, *The Iroquois.* Cambridge, MA: Blackwell, 1994, p. 80.
3. Quoted in Editors of Time-Life Books, *Realm of the Iroquois.* Alexandria, VA: Time-Life Books, 1993, p. 94.
4. Quoted in Lee Miller, ed., *From the Heart: Voices of the American Indian.* New York: Knopf, 1995, p. 78.
5. *Realm of the Iroquois*, p. 161.

Chapter 2: People of the Longhouse

6. Doug George-Kanentiio, "How Much Land Did the Iroquois Possess?" p. 60. www.ratical.org/many_worlds/6nations/HowMuchLand.html.
7. Quoted in W. Vernon Kinietz, *The Indians of the Western Great Lakes, 1615–1760.* Ann Arbor: University of Michigan Press, 1965, p. 242.
8. Quoted in *Realm of the Iroquois*, p. 36.
9. Quoted in Underhill, *Red Man's America*, p. 96.
10. Quoted in Underhill, *Red Man's America*, p. 83.
11. Underhill, *Red Man's America*, p. 97.
12. Quoted in Alan Axelrod, *Chronicle of the Indian Wars: From Colonial Times*

to *Wounded Knee.* New York: Prentice-Hall, 1993, p. 43.
13. Quoted in June Namias, *White Captives: Gender and Ethnicity on the American Frontier.* Chapel Hill: University of North Carolina Press, 1993, p. 175.
14. Namias, *White Captives*, p. 175.
15. Denise Lardner Carmody and John Tully Carmody, *Native American Religions.* New York: Paulist Press, 1993, p. 38.

Chapter 3: Religion and Ritual

16. Underhill, *Red Man's America*, p. 98.
17. Colin G. Calloway, *Indians of the Northeast.* New York: Facts On File, 1991, pp. 11–13.
18. Snow, *The Iroquois*, p. 159.
19. Ruth M. Underhill, *Red Man's Religion.* Chicago: University of Chicago Press, 1965, p. 181.
20. Underhill, *Red Man's Religion*, p. 177.
21. Snow, *The Iroquois*, p. 71.

Chapter 4: Political and Social Organization

22. Underhill, *Red Man's Religion*, p. 180.
23. Snow, *The Iroquois*, p. 72.
24. *Realm of the Iroquois*, p. 58.
25. Snow, *The Iroquois*, p. 57.
26. Snow, *The Iroquois*, pp. 55–56.
27. Carol Jacobs's presentation to the United Nations, as quoted in *Akwesasne Notes*

New Series, Fall 1995, pp. 116–17, reprinted in "The Six Nations: Oldest Living Participatory Democracy on Earth," www.ratical.org/many_worlds/6nations.

28. Quoted in *Realm of the Iroquois*, p. 47.

29. Quoted in Laurence M. Hauptman, "Designing Woman: Minnie Kellogg, Iroquois Leader," in L. G. Moses and Raymond Wilson, eds., *Indian Lives: Essays on Nineteenth- and Twentieth-Century Native American Leaders*. Albuquerque: University of New Mexico Press, 1993, p. 163.

30. Oren Lyons, "American Indian in the Past," in *Exiled in the Land of the Free*. Santa Fe: Clear Light Publishers, 1992, p. 39.

31. Quoted in Paul A. Wallace, *The White Roots of Peace*. Saranack Lake, NY: Chauncy Press, 1986, p. 43.

32. Lyons, "American Indian in the Past," p. 33.

33. Quoted in Axelrod, *Chronicle of the Indian Wars*, p. 41.

34. Quoted in *Realm of the Iroquois,* pp. 55–56.

35. Lyons, "American Indian in the Past," p. 32.

Chapter 5: The Coming of the White Man

36. *Realm of the Iroquois*, p. 55.

37. Francis Jennings, *The Founders of America*. W. W. Norton, 1993, p. 182.

38. Quoted in Jennings, *The Founders of America*, p. 197.

39. George R. Hamell, quoted in Jennings, *The Founders of America*, p. 182.

40. Quoted in *Realm of the Iroquois*, p. 83.

41. Francis Jennings, *The Ambiguous Iroquois Empire*. New York: W. W. Norton, 1984, p. 85.

42. Reader's Digest Editors, *Through Indian Eyes: The Untold Story of Native American Peoples*. Pleasantville, NY: Reader's Digest, 1995, p. 137.

43. Underhill, *Red Man's America*, p. 103.

44. Letter from Jaques Bruhyas, Jan. 21, 1668, quoted in Jennings, *The Ambiguous Iroquois Empire*, p. 95.

45. James Wilson, *The Earth Shall Weep: A History of Native America*. New York: Atlantic Monthly Press, 1998, p. 114.

46. Axelrod, *Chronicle of the Indian Wars*, p. 68.

47. Douglas Edward Leach, *The Northern Colonial Frontier: 1607–1763*. New York: Holt, Rinehart, and Winston, 1966, p. 104.

48. Quoted in Miller, *From the Heart*, p. 84.

49. Jennings, *The Founders of America*, p. 214.

50. Leach, *The Northern Colonial Frontier*, p. 108.

Chapter 6: The Confederacy Unravels

51. Sadekanaktie, quoted in Reader's Digest Editors, *Through Indian Eyes*, p. 131.

52. Leach, *The Northern Colonial Frontier*, p. 121.

53. H. A. Vernon, "Maris Bryant Pierce: The Making of a Seneca Leader," in Moses and Wilson, *Indian Lives,* pp. 19–20.

54. Snow, *The Iroquois*, p. 142.

55. Quoted in Axelrod, *Chronicle of the Indian Wars*, p. 55.

56. Leach, *The Northern Colonial Frontier*, p. 117.

57. Snow, *The Iroquois*, p. 134.

58. Quoted in Jennings, *The Founders of America*, p. 299.

59. Quoted in Miller, *From the Heart*, p. 102.

60. Quoted in Reader's Digest Editors, *Through Indian Eyes*, p. 145.

61. Quoted in Miller, *From the Heart*, pp. 101–102.

62. Axelrod, *Chronicle of the Indian Wars*, p. 109.

63. Quoted in Axelrod, *Chronicle of the Indian Wars*, p. 105.

64. Quoted in Reader's Digest Editors, *Through Indian Eyes*, p. 146.

65. Quoted in Jennings, *The Founders of America*, p. 301.

66. Quoted in Wilson, *The Earth Shall Weep*, p. 130.

67. Quoted in Reader's Digest Editors, *Through Indian Eyes*, p. 148.

Chapter 7: Decline and Renewal

68. Quoted in Reader's Digest Editors, *Through Indian Eyes*, p. 140.

69. Jennings, *The Ambiguous Iroquois Empire*, p. 9.

70. Quoted in Reader's Digest Editors, *Through Indian Eyes,* p. 140.

71. John Mason, quoted in Lyons, "American Indian in the Past," p. 26.

72. Quoted in Vernon, "Maris Bryant Pierce," p. 28.

73. Quoted in Reader's Digest Editors, *Through Indian Eyes*, p. 138.

74. Snow, *The Iroquois*, p. 156.

75. Wilson, *The Earth Shall Weep*, p. 131.

76. Quoted in Reader's Digest Editors, *Through Indian Eyes*, p. 338.

77. Quoted in Hauptman, "Designing Woman," p. 164.

78. Quoted in Wilson, *The Earth Shall Weep*, p. 299.

79. Quoted in Wilson, *The Earth Shall Weep*, p. 303.

80. Quoted in William Dudley, ed., *Native Americans: Opposing Viewpoints*. San Diego: Greenhaven Press, 1998, p. 181.

Chapter 8: Adaptation and Tradition

81. Quoted in Wilson, *The Earth Shall Weep*, p. 427.

82. Quoted in Reader's Digest Editors, *Through Indian Eyes*, p. 356.

83. Quoted in Wilson, *The Earth Shall Weep*, p. 342.

84. Quoted in Dudley, *Native Americans*, p. 203.

85. Quoted in Wilson, *The Earth Shall Weep*, p. 342.

86. Quoted in Wilson, *The Earth Shall Weep*, p. 347.

87. Quoted in Calloway, *Indians of the Northeast*, p. 82.

88. Wilson, *The Earth Shall Weep*, p. 417.

89. Quoted in Wilson, *The Earth Shall Weep*, p. 427.

90. Snow, *The Iroquois*, p. 221.

91. Quoted in Wilson, *The Earth Shall Weep*, p. 427.

For Further Reading

Susan Avery and Linda Skinner, *Extraordinary American Indians.* Chicago: Childrens Press, 1992. A series of short biographical sketches of famous American Indians, including several Iroquois, from the early days of European contact to today.

Nancy Bonvillain, *Hiawatha: Founder of the Iroquois Confederacy.* New York: Chelsea House, 1992. Written by a renowned anthropologist, this biography of the life of the Onondaga leader focuses particular attention on his skill as an orator and negotiator and his success in uniting independent nations.

Nancy Bonvillain, *The Mohawk.* New York: Chelsea House, 1992. A discussion of the life and times of the "People of the Place of the Flint," from pre-European contact to the present.

Esther K. Braun and David P. Braun, *The First Peoples of the Northeast.* Lincoln, MA: Moccasin Hill, 1994. Based on archaeological research, this book for general audiences covers twelve thousand years of the history of the native peoples of New York, New England, and the Canadian Maritimes. Publication was supported by the Massachusetts Archaeological Society.

Colin G. Calloway, *Indians of the Northeast.* New York: Facts On File, 1991. An illustrated history of the Native Americans who occupied what is now the northeastern United States, from ancient times to the present.

Barbara Graymont, *The Iroquois.* New York: Chelsea House, 1988. An excellent account of the Iroquois, chronicling their history, heritage, and culture.

Barbara Graymont, *The Iroquois and the American Revolution.* Syracuse, NY: University of Syracuse Press, 1972. A description of the role that the Iroquois played in the events leading up to and during the American Revolution.

Diane Hoyt-Goldsmith, *Lacrosse: The National Game of the Iroquois*. New York: Holiday House, 1998. A pictorial history of this most famous Iroquois game and the importance it still holds for the Iroquois.

Lawrence C. Kelly, *Federal Indian Policy*. New York: Chelsea House, 1990. Follows the course of relations between Native American groups and the United States government from 1790 until 1990.

Sharon Malinowski and Simon Glickman, eds., *Native North American Biography*. New York: UXL, 1996. Two volumes of short, easy-to-read biographical accounts of noteworthy historical and contemporary Native Americans.

Megan McClard and George Ypsilantis, *Hiawatha and the Iroquois League*. Englewood Cliffs, NJ: Silver Burdett, 1989. An easy-to-read account of Hiawatha's life, legend, and legacy, focusing on his contribution to peaceful government among his people.

Edwin Tunis, *Indians*. New York: Thomas Y. Crowell, 1979. An illustrated re-creation of American Indian life before the arrival of the white man; in addition to introductory chapters focusing on Indians as a whole, one chapter is devoted to the Iroquois.

Works Consulted

Books

George H. J. Abrams, *The Seneca People*. Phoenix: Indian Tribal Series, 1976. A short account of the history of the Seneca nation.

Alan Axelrod, *Chronicle of the Indian Wars: From Colonial Times to Wounded Knee*. New York: Prentice-Hall, 1993. A history of the wars between Indians and the white man, relying heavily on firsthand sources, including diaries and letters of military commanders, captivity narratives and missionary journals, army reports, treaties, and Native American oral accounts.

Denise Lardner Carmody and John Tully Carmody, *Native American Religions*. New York: Paulist Press, 1993. Written for university students, an introductory guide to the religions of the American Indians.

William Dudley, ed., *Native Americans: Opposing Viewpoints*. San Diego: Greenhaven Press, 1998. A series of essays, compiled for high school students, regarding views toward and policies affecting American Indians, from colonial days to the present.

Editors of Time-Life Books, *Realm of the Iroquois*. Alexandria, VA: Time-Life Books, 1993. An easy-to-read book that chronicles the life of the Iroquois nations, from the time that the five nations came together to forge an alliance to the present day. Includes lots of photographs, maps, and artifacts.

Editors of Time-Life Books, *The Spirit World*. Alexandria, VA: Time-Life Books, 1992. An easy-to-read book that describes the spiritual life of the Native Americans. Includes photographs, maps, and artifacts.

Francis Jennings, *The Ambiguous Iroquois Empire*. New York: W. W. Norton, 1984. A scholarly historical account of the complex alliance of tribes and colonies of the Covenant Chain, focusing particular attention on the role of the Iroquois in the development of colonial America.

Francis Jennings, *The Founders of America*. W. W. Norton, 1993. Describes the multitude of cultures and societies present in pre-European America and the effects of the European invasion on these cultures.

Bruce E. Johansen, *Forgotten Founders: Benjamin Franklin, the Iroquois and the Rationale for the American Revolution*. Ipswich, MA: Gambit, 1982. Describes the influence of the Native American thought and practices on the American mind, arguing that the Indians played a substantial role in defining principles and ideas of the American Revolution and the U.S. Constitution.

Alvin M. Josephy Jr., *The Indian Heritage of America*. Boston: Houghton Mifflin, 1991. A comprehensive account of the history and culture of Native American life in North America, from the prehistoric peoples of the Ice Age to the end of the twentieth century. Discusses similarities and differences among various tribes as it seeks to replace stereotypes with a true portrait of American Indians as they were and are.

Michael Kammen, *Colonial New York: A History*. White Plains, New York: kto press, 1975. A history of the colony of New York, including the story of the Indians who lived there.

W. Vernon Kinietz, *The Indians of the Western Great Lakes, 1615–1760*. Ann Arbor: University of Michigan Press, 1965. A classic treatment of the Native American lifestyle during the time of the first European contact.

Douglas Edward Leach, *The Northern Colonial Frontier: 1607–1763*. New York: Holt, Rinehart, and Winston, 1966. A history of the white settlement of New York and surrounding areas, focusing particular attention on the interactions with the indigenous peoples of the region.

Oren Lyons et al., *Exiled in the Land of the Free*. Santa Fe: Clear Light Publishers, 1992. A series of essays, written by contemporary experts on Native American history and culture, regarding the influence of American Indians on American thought and culture.

Lee Miller, ed., *From the Heart: Voices of the American Indian.* New York: Knopf, 1995. An anthology of speeches of Native Americans yields a compelling oral history of America from the sixteenth through nineteenth centuries as experienced by the natives of the continent.

L. G. Moses and Raymond Wilson, eds., *Indian Lives: Essays on Nineteenth- and Twentieth-Century Native American Leaders.* Albuquerque: University of New Mexico Press, 1993. Short biographies of Native Americans written by authoritative sources. Two essays focus on Iroquois leaders: H. A. Vernon's "Maris Bryant Pierce: The Making of a Seneca Leader," and Laurence M. Hauptman's "Designing Woman: Minnie Kellogg, Iroquois Leader."

June Namias, *White Captives: Gender and Ethnicity on the American Frontier.* Chapel Hill: University of North Carolina Press, 1993. A compilation of the stories of Euro-Americans who were captured by Indians during the eighteenth and nineteenth centuries and an analysis of what their experiences indicate about Indian-white relations on the American frontier.

Reader's Digest Editors, *Through Indian Eyes: The Untold Story of Native American Peoples.* Pleasantville, NY: Reader's Digest, 1995. The history of America as experienced by Native Americans, amplified by illustrations and by memorable quotations from native people, past and present.

Dean R. Snow, *The Iroquois.* Cambridge, MA: Blackwell, 1994. A scholarly account of the history of the Iroquois from A.D. 900 to the present.

Ruth M. Underhill, *Red Man's America.* Chicago: University of Chicago Press, 1971. A comprehensive study of North American Indian societies, beginning with the first migrations from Siberia and following their subsequent migration southward and eastward.

Ruth M. Underhill, *Red Man's Religion.* Chicago: University of Chicago Press, 1965. A companion to *Red Man's America*, this book gives an overview of the spiritual beliefs and ceremonies of Native Americans north of Mexico.

Paul A. Wallace, *The White Roots of Peace.* Saranack Lake, NY: Chauncy Press, 1986. In this classic, Wallace retells the epic of Deganawidah, the Peacemaker, the charismatic spiritual leader who united warring tribes of the Northeast to form the Iroquois Confederacy.

James Wilson, *The Earth Shall Weep: A History of Native America*. New York: Atlantic Monthly Press, 1998. Accessible to a broad audience, this historical account of Native American life charts the collision course between indigenous cultures, paying particular attention to the Native American perspective.

The World of the American Indian. Washington, DC: National Geographic, 1989. Details the history and cultural traditions of Native American tribes.

Internet Sources

Rekha Balu, "Indian Identity: Who's Drawing the Boundaries?" American Bar Association, 1999. www.abanet.org/genpractice/compleat/f95identity.html.

Doug George-Kanentiio, "How Much Land Did the Iroquois Possess?" www.ratical.org/many_worlds/6nations/HowMuchLand.html.

Hartford Web Publishing, World History Archives, "The Constitution of the Iroquois Nations," 1999. www.hartford-hwp.com/archives/41/036.html.

Onondaga Historical Association Research Center, "Indian Magna Carta Writ In Wampum Belts," by Howard McLellan, reprinted from the *New York Times*, June 7, 1925, in *Akwesasne Notes New Series*, Fall 1995. www.ratical.org.many_worlds/6nations/WampumBelts.html.

The Seneca Nation of Indians, "The Canandaigua Treaty of 1794," 1999. http://home.netscape.com/comprod/mirror/index.html.

Websites

The Seneca Nation of Indians. www.sni.org. The home page of the Seneca includes information about the three reservations to which the Seneca hold the title; the Canandaigua Treaty of 1794, which gave them title to this land; current news; and other information about the nation's cultural resources, government, education, etc.

The Cayuga Nation of the Six Nations of the Grand River Territory. http://tuscaroras.com/cayuganation. This website provides information on the formation of the Iroquois Confederacy and the significance of "Hiawatha's Belt."

Index

Picture Credits

Cover photo: Michael S. Yamashita/Corbis
Archive Photos, 14, 17, 38, 47, 59, 64, 68, 77
©Nathan Benn/Corbis, 11, 33
©Bettmann/Corbis, 16, 19, 86, 91
©N. Carter/North Wind, 26
©Richard A. Cooke/Corbis, 39
©Corbis, 69, 84
©Kevin Fleming/Corbis, 71
FPG International, 93
Library of Congress, 46, 54, 79
North Wind, 9, 44, 45, 56, 57
©Phil Schermeister/Corbis, 92
©Lee Snider/Corbis, 74
©Paul A. Souders/Corbis, 29, 89
©Ted Spiegel/Corbis, 51
©Stock Montage, Inc., 23, 30
©Michael S. Yamashita/Corbis, 35

About the Author

Lydia Bjornlund is a private consultant and freelance writer, focusing primarily on issues related to civic education, government, and training. She is the author of more than a dozen books and training manuals, as well as numerous magazine and newsletter articles.

Ms. Bjornlund holds a master of education degree from Harvard University and a bachelor of arts from Williams College, where she majored in American studies. She lives in Oakton, Virginia, with her husband, Gerry Hoetmer, and their brand new twins Jake and Sophia.